THE
LEGACY OF WISDOM

A Handbook of
American Indian Heritage

William Marder

THE BOOK TREE
San Diego, California

ISBN 978-1-58509-150-8

Cover layout
Mike Sparrow

Cover art
provided by William Marder,
which shows the great Chief Joseph of the Nez Perce tribe,
also known as Hin-mah-too-yah-lat-kekt, or
Thunder Rolling Down the Mountain

Legacy of Wisdom for All to Follow

Care for Mother Earth and Father Sky
Protect and Nurture Our Children and Youth
Question and Resist All Stereotypes
Care and Respect Your Elders
Reject All of "Manifest Destiny"
Slow Down and Listen More than You Talk
Live With Gratitude
Live Lightly On the Earth
Work to End Global Warming
Support Renewable Energy
Stop Hydrofracking, Dirty Coal and
Uranium Mining
Learn and Respect Your Tribal Cultures
Remember that All Beings - Animals & Plants
Are Your Relatives, Not Your Resources
Appreciate and Learn about the Diversity
of Nations, Cultures and All People
Give Thanks Frequently
Consider Future Generations in All Your Actions

DEDICATED TO

our new great grandson, Jonah Ellis Kleinman, born April 25,
2016 as a part of the coming seventh generation.

ACKNOWLEDGEMENTS

Eric Barasch for excellent computer help. Dolores Kaufman for
her fabulous editing and advice. Estelle Marder for her patience.

ABOUT THE AUTHOR

William (Bill) Marder has had a
photographic career of over 60 years, which
includes inventing new techniques involved
with color printing and winning numerous
awards. His other related book from 2004,
Indians In The Americas: The Untold Story,
received excellent reviews for gathering
together and revealing the true history of
American Indians. With over 20 years of
research behind it, it details extensive facts not found in standard
textbooks and many photos never before seen or published until
now. He considers this handbook to be a more action-oriented
companion volume, which uses truth from the past in order to
help people today.

CONTENTS

INTRODUCTION

This is an additional work related to my book *Indians In the Americas: The Untold Story*, published in 2005. The first book covers tribal histories, while this one is a personal guidebook.

Why am I still involved and attracted to the American Indians as well as all indigenous people and their former ways of life? In simple terms, it is their spiritual philosophy of respecting one another as well as other people, whoever they are. With the passing of over 10 years since my last book on American Indians I have found that most of their lives have drastically worsened.

With the entrance of the white man to the New World, the lives of the American Indians and the restrictions placed on their culture, and on their offspring, robbed them of their rightful and beautiful heritage. Life has changed dramatically from the time Christopher Columbus first landed in the Americas in 1492 and wrote in his journal on his meeting with the American Indians on November 11, 1492, "I see and know that these people have no religion, nor are they idolaters, but rather, meek and know no evil, that they do not kill or capture others and are without weapons." Yet, Columbus, his men, the Spanish empire, and the succeeding Dutch, English, French etc., invaders to this land of theirs, then went about with their cannons and attack dogs etc. creating the worst holocaust (genocide) ever witnessed by killing, enslaving, raping, and almost annihilating the American Indians and their way of life. The population for American Indians before Columbus in the Americas was estimated at about 50 to 75 million by independent researchers. In the 1910 census, after all the genocidal massacres, only 265,683 remained, including mixed bloods. Today, their population throughout all of the Americas is approximately 60 million. All this genocide was for gold and anything else of value the invaders could steal that have presently ended up at the top tier of one percent of our modern day society. The rest of us are left with what trickled down from the top. We have gained only material riches, while entire countries and people are destroyed by continual wars, famine, climate change, and pollution. With all this, all we have left our children is the future forecast for the destruction of our entire planet, according to our scientific community.

I've found that the present generation of Native American youth in their everyday lives are drastically feeling the effects of being penned in on a reservation with no hope. At present, many of the tribes in both the United States and Canada are barely able to survive, penned in on their reservation prisons with over 80% unemployment, crime, drugs and alcohol destroying the people, along with an epidemic of suicides in both children and adults as well as inadequate, underfunded health care. All their culture, dreams, and hopes have been shattered.

The past beliefs of American Indian tribes were based on being in balance with nature. The Indian tribes were not wasteful. They never took more than what nature could restore. Even tribal structure was in balance. If someone was in need there was always someone willing to give. Generosity was an admirable trait. Hoarding more property than needed was looked down upon. The information below varied with each tribe, but was similar. These tribes were given false names by their colonizers, as well as the name American Indian, which I use in this book. More information can be found in my other book, *Indians In The Americas, The Untold Story*.[1]

Please carry this book with you as a reference to the great heritage and culture of Native Americans.

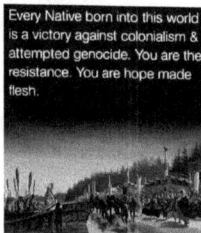

Every Native born into this world is a victory against colonialism & attempted genocide. You are the resistance. You are hope made flesh.

THE LEGACY OF WISDOM

RELIGION: American Indian religious beliefs were centered around the tribes' interpretation of a creator that was given different names. The Plains Indians believed in the Great Spirit or Wakan Tanka. Religion was part of everyday life for the Sioux. They believed everything had a spirit. The Indians believed that the Great Spirit had power over all things including animals, trees, stones, and clouds. Wakan-Tanka is at the center of the universe, which is everywhere and within every person. This is the fervent belief that is at the heart of all American Indian customs, which also includes Father Sky, Great Spirit Mother, and Mother Earth. The earth was believed to be the mother of all spirits. The sun also had great power because it gave the Earth light and warmth. The Plains Indians prayed individually and in groups. They believed that visions in dreams came from the spirits. There were underwater spirits that controlled all animals and plants. High in the sky, they believed there were spirits called Thunderbirds. The Thunderbirds were the most powerful spirits except for the Great Spirit, who was the most powerful of all. The Great Spirit was the Lakota (Sioux) Creator. Another spirit, The White Buffalo Woman, gave each tribe a sacred pipe. They called these pipes "Medicine Pipes." When lit, smokers might be able to have a vision. Visions were powerful things. They believed that dreams and visions were ways to talk to the spirits.

To most of us, the mention of religion brings to mind notions of God, a supreme over-ruler, and a decidedly personal being. Nothing like this is found among the Indians. Yet they seem to have formulated rather complex and abstract notions of a controlling power, or series of powers, pervading the universe. Thus, the Dakota use a term Wakan Tanka, which seems to mean the "greatest sacred one." The term has often been rendered as the "Great Mystery," but that is not quite correct.

It is true that anything strange and mysterious is pronounced Wakan, or as having attributes analogous to Wakan Tanka, which seems to mean supernatural. In fact, the Dakota do recognize a kind of hierarchy in which the Sun stands first, as one of the Wakan Tanka. Of almost equal rank are the Sky, the Earth, and the Rock. Next in order, is another group of four—the Moon (female), Winged-One, Wind, and the "Mediator" (female). Then come inferior beings: the buffalo, bear, the four winds and the whirlwind; then come four classes or groups of beings and so on, in almost bewildering complexity. So far as we know, no other Plains tribe has worked out quite so complex a conception. The Omaha Wakonda is, in a way, like the Dakota Wakan Tanka. The Pawnee recognized a dominating power spoken of as Tirawa, or " father," under whom were the heavenly bodies, the winds, the thunder, lightning, and rain; but they also recognized a sacred quality, or presence, in the phenomena of the world, spoken of as Kawaharu, a term whose meaning closely parallels the Dakota Wakan. The Blackfoot resolved the phenomena of the universe into "powers," the greatest and most universal of which is Natosiwa, or Sun power. The Sun was, in a way, a personal god having the moon for his wife and the Morning Star for his son. All told, the American Indian tribes were aware of an all-pervading force or element in the universe that emanates from an indefinite source, to which a special name was given by their tribe. Probably nowhere, not even among the Dakota, is there a clear-cut formulation of a definite god-like being with definite powers and functions. [2]

SUPERNATURAL HELPER: With the Plains Indians, as well as in some other parts of the indigenous world, the ideal is for all males to establish some kind of direct relation with a divine element or power. The idea is that if one follows the proper formula, the power will appear in some human or animal form and will form a compact with the young man for his good fortune during life. Generally, the youth will put himself in the hands of a priest, or shaman, who instructs him and requires him to fast and pray alone in some secluded spot until a vision or dream is obtained. In the Plains, such an experience results in the conferring of one or more songs, the laying on of certain curious formal taboos, and of the designation of some object, such as a feather, skin, or shell, to be carried and used as a charm or medicine bundle. This practice has been reported for the Sarsi, Plains-Cree, Blackfoot, Gros Ventre, Crow, Hidatsa, Mandan, Dakota Sioux, Assiniboine, Omaha, Arapaho, Cheyenne, Kiowa, and Pawnee. It is probably universal except perhaps among the Ute, Shoshone, and Nez Perce. We know also that it is frequent among the Woodland Cree, Menomini, and Ojibway.

11

Aside from hunger and thirst, there was no self-torture except among the Dakota, and possibly a few others of Siouan stock. With these, it was the rule for all desiring to become shamans, or those in close rapport with the divine element, to thrust skewers through the skin and tie themselves up as in the Sun Dance. When a Blackfoot, Dakota, or an Omaha went out to fast and pray for a revelation, he called upon all the recognized mythical creatures, the heavenly bodies, and all in the earth and in the waters which are consistent with the tribes' conceptions of power. If this divine element spoke through a hawk, for example, the young man would then look upon that bird as his Wakonda. He would then keep, in a bundle, the skin or feathers of a hawk so that the divine presence might ever be at hand. This is why the warriors of the Plains carried such charms into battle and looked to them for aid. We define the religion of the American Indians as a group of concepts and acts which spring from the relation of the individual to the outer world. The scope of religious concepts

Medicine Man with sacred bundle

Shaman Giving his Blessings

depends, to a certain extent, on the knowledge of the laws of nature and, since the natural and the supernatural, as conceived in the mind of American Indians, does not coincide with our view of this subject, there are marked differences in the scope of religion. For instance, the causal relations determining the movements of the stars are now recognized by civilized man but, at an earlier time, it was believed that the positions of the stars influenced the fates of man in a mysterious manner, and that their movements could be controlled by his will. Among tribes which held to the latter opinion, views relating to the heavenly bodies would form part of the religion of the people; while among those peoples to which the causal relations determining the motions of the stars are known, these motions are no longer subject to religious interpretations. Although the belief of the American Indians in the powers of inanimate objects is common, we find that, on the whole, animals, particularly the larger ones, are most frequently considered as possessed of such magic power. [3]

BANNING OF RELIGIOUS RITES: The arrival of European settlers marked a major change in American Indian culture. Some of the first Europeans that the Indians would meet were often missionaries who looked upon American Indian spirituality practices as worthless superstition inspired by the Christian devil. These early missionaries then determined to convert the American Indians to Christianity. As more and more Europeans flooded North America, US and Canadian governments instituted policies to force Natives onto the majority culture. Beginning in 1882, the Federal Government, in order to encourage those on reservations to become assimilated into European culture, began to work towards banning American Indian religious rights, which impacted their spiritual traditions. At that time, U.S. Interior Secretary Henry M. Teller, ordered an end to all "heathenish dances and ceremonies" on reservations due to their "great hindrance to civilization." This was further supported the following year by Hiram Price, Commissioner of Indian Affairs, when his 1883 report stated: "...there is no good reason why an Indian should be permitted to indulge in practices which are alike repugnant to common decency and morality; and the preservation of good order on the reservations demands some active measures should be taken to discourage and, if possible, put a stop to the demoralizing influence of heathenish rites."

Ghost Dance 1890

Wounded Knee Massacre Dec. 1890

These attempts to suppress the traditions of American Indians eventually led to the Massacre at Wounded Knee on December 29, 1890, when the government attempted to stop the practice of the "Ghost Dance," based originally on the circle dance, a traditional dance that has been used by many indigenous people since prehistoric times. The Ghost Dance in 1890 was a far-reaching movement that prophesied a peaceful end to white American expansion and preached goals of clean living, an honest life, and cross-cultural cooperation by all American Indians. When the Seventh U.S. Calvary was sent into the Lakota Sioux's Pine Ridge and Rosebud Reservations to stop the

Cheyenne Medicine Man

dance and arrest the participants, approximately 150 Native American men, women, and children were killed. Though charges of killing innocents were brought against members of the Seventh Calvary, all were exonerated. Just two years later, further measures were taken to suppress Native religions, when Commissioner of Indian Affairs Thomas J. Morgan ordered penalties of up to six months in prison for those who repeatedly participated in religious dances or acted as medicine men.

However, these new laws were almost impossible to enforce and the Native Americans continued their customs. Though some traditions were lost along the way, many others survived despite the ban, and various tribes continue to follow many spiritual traditions. Some American Indians have been devout Christians for generations, and their practices today combine their traditional customs with Christian elements. Other tribes, particularly in the Southwest, have retained their aboriginal traditions, mostly intact. Amazingly, the ban against American Indian spiritual rituals continued to be in place until the 1978 passage of the American Indian Religious Freedom Act. Today, many tribes continue to guard the knowledge of their medicine people and will not discuss the topic with non-Indians. Some believe that sharing healing knowledge will weaken the spiritual power of the medicine." [4]

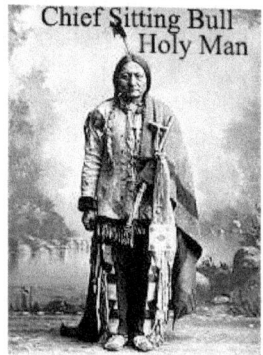
Chief Sitting Bull Holy Man

MEDICINE MAN (SHAMAN): A medicine man or medicine woman is a traditional healer and spiritual leader among the American Indians and Indigenous peoples of North America and other parts of the world. The medicine they use refers to the combined health practices of over 500 distinct nations that inhabited the Americas before the European arrival at the end of the fifteenth century. Specific practices varied among tribes, but all native medicine is based on the understanding that man is part of nature and health is a matter of balance. American Indian philosophy recognizes aspects of the natural world that cannot be seen by the eye or by technology, but which can be experienced directly and intuitively. Just as each human has an immeasurable inner life which powerfully influences well-being, so does nature include unseen but compelling forces which must be addressed and integrated for true balance to be achieved. The Medicine Man or Shaman is trained in healing the sick and interpreting signs and dreams. Techniques commonly used include self-inquiry to identify what needs to be changed, lifestyle modification, herbs (echinacea, goldenseal, burdock root and sage, among others), prayer, various types of massage, and ceremonies such as the sweat lodge and vision quest. There was (or is) usually only one medicine man per tribe. The medicine man performed ceremonies. Each ceremony usually honored one spirit at a time.

The Arctic people are closely connected to nature. Their tradition believes that every being has a spirit and must be treated with respect. The Mandans, like members of other tribes, tried to live in a relationship of respect with the land and with nonhuman life. Daily life and special occasions required rituals meant to create a correct relationship with the supernatural. Men and women fasted and offered sacrifices to gain the protection of supernatural protectors.

Navajo Medicine Men using sand painting for healing

The Mandan Okipa (or Sun Dance) included fasting and self-piercing and is a four-day powerful religious ceremony. Certain tribal members held sacred bundles, which might belong either to an individual or to the tribe as a whole. These sacred bundles held items of symbolic significance. Maintaining and caring for a bundle was a complicated process, and children who might expect to inherit one someday began learning how to maintain the bundle at a young age. Although the Mandans belonged to matrilineal clans, the bundles were passed down to the eldest male heirs of these clans. Sweat lodges were used to cleanse and purify the body and soul. The sweat lodge was created by forming long wooden poles into a dome. Buffalo hides or canvas were used to make an airtight seal, covering the dome.

There was an alter made a few feet from the door, which usually consisted of a buffalo skull mounted on a small mound. Also, rocks would be heated in a fire pit in front of the lodge until they were glowing. When the rocks were ready, they were placed inside of the lodge, where a hole was dug in the middle.

Those participating in the ritual seat themselves around the interior of the lodge while different parts of the ceremony are carried out as they remained for an extended period, singing and praying together. [5]

Hu Kalawa Indian Altar, Photo 1907 by Edward S. Curtis
Slow Bull, Saliva, and Picket Pin, kneeling with bison skull

CLANS: A Clan is a group of people united by actual or perceived kinship and descent. Even if lineage details are unknown, clan members may be organized around a founding member or related to an ancestor. The kinship-based bonds may be symbolical, whereby the clan shares a "stipulated" common ancestor that is a symbol of the clan's unity. When this "ancestor" is non-human, it is referred to as a totem, which is frequently an animal. In other cultures and situations, a clan does not usually mean the same thing as other kin-based groups, such as tribes, and bands. Often, the distinguishing factor is that a clan is a smaller part of a larger society such as a chiefdom, or a state. In some societies, clans may have an official leader such as a chieftain or patriarch; in others, leadership positions may have to be achieved, or people may say that "elders" make decisions.

Generally the American Indian tribes can be divided into two categories, sedentary and nomadic. Sedentary farmers include the Hopi, the Zuni, the Yaqui and the Yuma. These tribes grew crops like corn, beans and squash. They lived in permanent settlements known as pueblos that were built of stone and adobe that resembled something like modern-day apartments. At their centers, many of these villages also had large ceremonial pit houses, or kivas. The other category is nomadic, including the Southwestern tribes such as the Lakota, called Sioux, – a derogatory name conferred on the group. The Sioux call themselves Lakota, Dakota or Nakota, which all mean "allies," but they also use the word Sioux in the present day. The Navajo and Apache tribes were known as hunters and gatherers.

Because these groups were always on the move, their homes were much less permanent than the pueblos. Most of the Indian tribes (of which there were many) were divided into clans or closely knit extended family groups, called "Tiyospaye" by the Western Lakota (Sioux). Indians lived in big families called clans. These clans were a group of relatives that had one common ancestor. The Cherokee Nation was divided into seven clans. A clan is a family of related people. The seven clans are: Long Hair, Paint, Bird, Wolf, Wild Potato, Deer, and Blue. When a child was born, he or she became a member of the mother's clan. Villages were a mix of clans. This was good because Cherokee law clearly stated that you could not marry someone from your own clan.

Totem poles were a very integral part of American Indian culture, primarily of the tribes in the Northwestern part of America. The Indians believed that each person was assigned the spirit of a particular animal and that their spirit was absorbed into this animal in death. The totem pole was a large, tall wooden carving of various animals, each representing a family member of a loved one who had passed away. The head of a clan at times is considered as the representative of the mythological ancestor of the clan, and as such, is believed to be endowed with superior powers. In this sense many of the political functions among Indian tribes are closely associated with what may be termed "priestly functions." The religious significance of social institutions is most clearly marked in cases where the tribes join in the performance of certain ceremonies, which serve a political or religious purpose. Such acts include inter-tribal ball games, the Busk of the Creek, the Sun Dance of the Plains Indians, and performances of numerous warrior societies. Here also belong the secret societies, which are highly developed among the Pueblos in California, and on the North Pacific coast. It is characteristic of some of these rituals to develop into dramatic representations of the myth from which the ritual is derived. For this reason the use of masks is a common feature in which certain individuals impersonate supernatural beings. [6]

To sustain the closeness of these clans, the American Indians initiated a Naming Ceremony. The timing of this ritual varies; some tribes perform the ceremony shortly after birth; other Tribes perform the ritual when the child is several years old. In either case this ritual is illustrative of formal kinship obligation. Naming ceremonies organize an obligatory, supportive network for children. Family members, such as uncles, aunts, or grandparents, are most often selected as namesakes, as well as names from nature or descriptive nicknames. In some tribes a newborn baby will receive a name, and when old enough to understand the meaning and importance of another name, he will receive that one. Names often tend to reflect a certain trait or strength in the person, and are often represented by an animal symbolizing those strengths. The name bestows certain powers and responsibilities. Highly trusted and reliable non-kin who have been incorporated into the family system may also serve as namesakes. Naming ceremonies revitalized an extended family system through organizing a social and spiritual fabric around those being cared for. [7]

HOUSING: Indians built many different types of homes because they lived in different climates and didn't have the same building materials. Some groups built large houses with many rooms where many families could stay together. Others had small dwellings in which only very few people lived. These were called Wigwam or Longhouses used by the Algonquian. Tipi (also tepee and teepee) is a Lakota name for a conical tent. Grass homes are thatched with prairie grass on a frame bent into a beehive by Southern plain tribes – wattle and daub houses (also known as asi) are the Cherokee words for them. Chickees (also known as chickee huts) are stilt houses or platform dwellings used by the Seminole Indians. Adobe houses (also known as pueblos) are used by the Pueblo Indians of the Southwest. Earthen house is a general term referring to several types of Native American homes, including Navajo hogans and Lakota earth lodges. Plank houses are homes used by tribes of the Northwest Coast (from northern California all the way up to Alaska). Igloos (or Iglu) are snow houses used by the Inuit (Eskimos) of northern Canada. Not all Inuit people used igloos – some built sod houses instead. The Inuit of Canada built snow

Eastern Longhouse

Hogan

.Adobe (Pueblo)   homes,Taos N. M

Tipi - tepee, teepee

houses during the winter, and in summer they lived in tents made of animal hides. In some parts of America Indians built wigwams that were covered with leaves. Some tribes built houses into the earth that they covered with leaves and grass. Indians of the Great Plains built tepees made of buffalo skin. The Pueblo Indians of the southwestern part of America used sun-dried bricks to make houses. Easily grown hemp as a building material has been put forward as an alternative to replace synthetic, petroleum based and other high-embodied energy materials to produce high performance building products that are better for the environment.[8]

Preparing Food

FOOD: The availability of natural food sources depended on the time of year. These times caused the Indian families to follow a semi-nomadic annual cycle of fishing, hunting, and gathering. This involved wintering at the

23

band's permanent village site, usually in a lower valley by a river. In spring there was root gathering, in summer there was salmon fishing, and in fall there was hunting and berry gathering. Originally the Lakota and Dakota Indians were corn farmers as well as hunters, but once they acquired horses they mostly gave up farming and moved frequently to follow the seasonal migrations of the buffalo herds. At the same time as they were being forced onto reservations, the buffalo were being slaughtered by the thousands. The U.S. military believed that if the buffalo could be eliminated, then the "Indian Problem" in America could be solved. The strategy proved to be successful and as the buffalo drew near extinction, the American Indian was also in danger of becoming extinct.

Mass Slaughter Buffalo Skulls

The American Indians diet was meat; especially buffalo, elk and deer, which they cooked in pits or dried and pounded into pemmican. The Sioux also collected chokecherries, fruit, and potatoes to eat. The Cherokee were farmers, hunters, and gatherers. They grew corn, squash, and beans along with pumpkin, melons, sunflowers, tobacco, and other crops. Corn was the most important food. The women made sure they planted enough crops to provide food for two years. Women had charge of cooking the daily meals, which usually were composed of maize, beans, and squash, plus whatever else was in season. Indians ate many different kinds of food. Those who lived on the plains of the Central United States ate the meat of buffalo. The Pueblos of the southwest lived on corn, beans and squash. Indians in Alaska and Canada were fishers and hunted deer and other wild animals in the forests. The Zunis were expert farming people. They raised crops of corn, beans, and squash, as well as cotton and tobacco.

Pueblo Bake Ovens

Zuni men also hunted deer, antelope, and small game, while women gathered nuts, fruits, and herbs. Favorite Zuni recipes included hominy, corn balls, baked beans, soups, and different types of cornbread. Most Indians ate berries and collected nuts. Indians cooked their food in ovens that they made with hot stones. They preserved meat by smoking or drying it in the sun.

The Maya ate very well. They hunted wild turkey, deer, ducks, and even monkey. They caught fish and ate bird eggs. They grew sweet potatoes, corn, beans, chilies, and squash. Corn was called maize. Out of all their foods, maize was the most important. They made corn flour and used it to make tortillas and other kinds of breads. Their foods changed with the seasons.

Food Gathering   Manoomin (Ojibwe) Wild Rice

In winter, they hunted birds and animals and lived on stored foods from the previous fall. In spring, they hunted, fished, and picked berries. In summer they grew crops (beans, corn, and squash). In fall they harvested crops and hunted for foods to preserve and keep for the winter. The American Indians used natural resources in every aspect of their lives. They used animal skins (deerskin) as clothing. Shelter was made from the material around them (saplings, leaves, small branches, animal fur). American Indians of the past farmed, hunted, and fished. They used natural resources such as rock, twine, bark, and oyster shell to farm, hunt, and fish. Women made and painted gourds for cooking and serving food. They also tended the kitchen garden and took care of the cattle. The kinds of food the American Indians ate, the clothing they wore, and the shelters they had depended upon the seasons.[9]

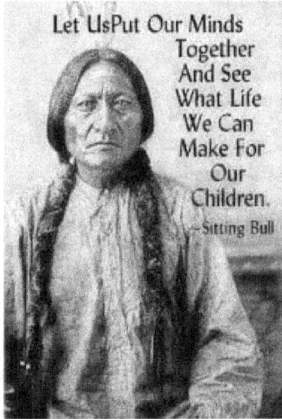

Let UsPut Our Minds Together And See What Life We Can Make For Our Children.
—Sitting Bull

CHILDREN: Children were considered an enormous asset in all the tribes, and the foundation of their tribe. The child was a sacred being given to them by their creator. Each child was entitled to a home, food, upbringing and education. A child was not property but a member of a large family and thus had rights. There was no such thing as an illegitimate child. Children were often taught at a young age to be strong and not show emotion. They were expected to conform to the ways of the tribe. Unlike many white children born with the Christian burden of original sin, the Indian child came into the world with divine qualities. Midwives and Medicine Women used their expertise with herbs to decrease or increase the woman's fertility. The mother readied herself for birth by eating sparingly and exercising. At birth the newborn baby was washed in cold water. A newborn infant was laid on it's back on a bed of soft material made up of the surrounding vegetation. Babies were nursed until they weaned themselves. They were carried close to the warmth of the body

The Ones that matter most are the Children. They are the true human beings.

during waking hours, at first by the mother, and later by their grandparents, aunts and older sisters. After a few months they were placed in a cradle-board and hung where they could watch their mother's activities. They were nursed

Mother teaching child
Basket Weaving

on demand, rocked by their mother or grandmother and soothed with lullabies. The grandmother held an honored position in the family. Young children and babies spent all of their time close to their mother. The mother would go about her daily work and chores carrying the baby on her back in a cradle-board. The mother often nursed the young child until it was two or three years old. Since the wife or wives were often busy with tasks, the small children were gently disciplined and watched over by the grandmother.

Since divorce was accepted and the raising of the child was the responsibility of many relatives, not just the biological mother and father, divorce does not appear to have had a negative impact on the children. In the early years girls and boys played together, but soon the boys were interested in their father's

Teaching the Children

occupations and the girl's would imitate their mothers. The children were all educated simply by observing. Children learned from their parents, uncles, and aunts. Girls helped their mothers. Boys helped their fathers. Both played games to strengthen their bodies and skills. At one point a boy went to live with his maternal uncle, who began teaching him to endure hardships of various kinds. The uncle also taught him hunting, magic, and the traditions of his clan and lineage.[10] Young members of the tribe from childhood up were advised by their grandparents who also gave them their original names.

YOUNG WOMEN: A young Indian girl's passage to womanhood was much different with the American Indians than with the Christians (and in a few other religions) in their belief that menstruation was a biblical curse. Basing their beliefs on the bible, European Christians believed that if a woman wasn't pregnant she wasn't in her natural state. The uncleanness of women entered Church Law especially through the Decretum Gratiani (1140 AD), which became official Church law in 1234 AD. In contrast, the Indians believed that menstruation is a beautiful celebration of life and that the bleeding time is strongly tied to the moon.

A woman's capacity for other worldly powers stemmed from her ability to bleed, oftentimes profusely. Some tribes actually believed that women were the embodiment of a holy person during their periods. Others believed that women's bodies were purifying themselves during this time. Perhaps most fascinating of all, is that many tribes believed women were more powerful, spiritually, during their periods – and that they even had special intuitive powers. American Indian puberty rituals were big celebratory events for a village. Early European settlers noted that the Cheyenne and Apache tribes were particularly open about menstruation, often announcing a girl's first period to the entire village with pride. In the Navajo tradition the girls participate in a run towards the rising sun. If a girl that is bleeding for the first time outruns everyone she is believed to have a good life. She is a strong woman. Some of the tribes, like Nootka in Canada, have a different kind of an endurance ritual. A girl is taken in a boat into the middle of the lake and left there. If she manages to swim back she is a woman ready to bear the pain, such as childbearing. In the Apache tradition a girl who is menstruating for the first time is called a "Changing Woman," and after a ceremony she gains the name of a "White Painted Woman." American Indian tribal members would call upon menstruating women for their advice, insight, guidance, or to connect them to higher powers. Menstrual huts were also big among most of the American Indian tribes. During the heaviest four days of their period, wives would leave their homes and go to this separate menstrual lodge to commune with other women.

Since women tend to have their menstruation together, these lodges were often quite full and the women inside were encouraged to engage in some serious "girl time" by discussing female issues and indulging in creative pursuits like storytelling and arts and crafts. In many American Indian tribes, menstruation involved a strong oral tradition, rituals, ceremonies and more. While women might have been restricted from cooking or sleeping with men during her period, this had nothing to do with shame. In fact, many Native American women were treated with an amazing amount of reverence when they were menstruating.

Kalispel woman

During this time her father's sister and other female relatives taught her the traditions of the clan. Chastity was so ingrained into their culture and belief system that they would not even look directly at a member of the opposite sex that was not a family member, and they were given few opportunities to be alone with potential suitors.

WOMEN: The American Indian women in the past could never imagine the abuse, or the traumas that the women of today face. She lived in a time when all walked in balance with all things. There was no domestic violence, no rape, no chauvinism, no oppression and no genocide. The Europeans, particularly the missionaries, had a great deal of difficulty in understanding that women in Indian society had certain powers.

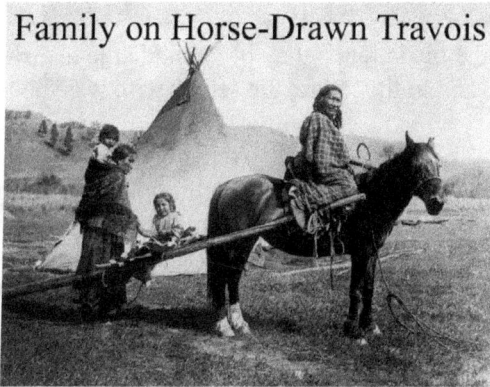

Family on Horse-Drawn Travois

One of the worst atrocities committed by the missionaries as they tried to (so-called) "civilize" the Indians was the degrading, upheaval, and removal of the power of the women. Most American Indian societies were not organized on the patriarchal, monogamous norms of European society. Although the woman played a subordinate role in ceremonial life and lacked formal political power (one will look in vain for a Plains Indian woman's signature on a treaty with the United States), they had the type of political power that contemporary American women lacked. For example they owned the lodge, tipi (also called tepee and teepee) and its contents (the fields, seeds, and implements of production), and the right to trade their

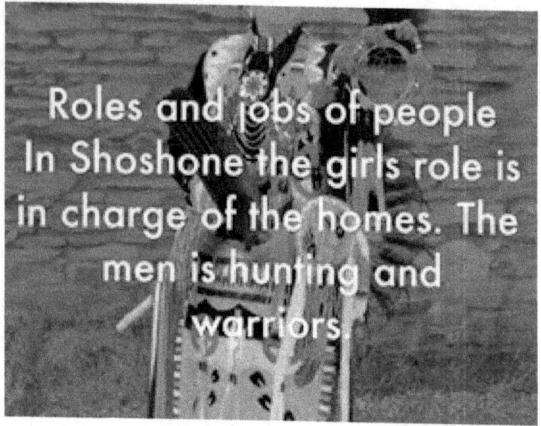

Roles and jobs of people In Shoshone the girls role is in charge of the homes. The men is hunting and warriors.

surplus crops. On the bison hunts they often made the decision on where to camp, and in the lodge, the senior wife was the main decision maker.

Women also had the right to divorce. And since they owned the lodge, an unkind husband could find himself homeless with only his horse and weapons to his name. Women were also held in high esteem for their craft work and played an important role in healing, especially in problems associated with childbirth. They take care of religious items, an important responsibility.

Marriages could be dissolved without ceremony and divorce for the woman in the Lakota (Sioux) tribe was easy; if she was unhappy with her husband she was allowed to throw all his possessions into the village circle to show the marriage was at an end. The Hopi Pueblo tribe taught their children that their mother's side must be favored as she bears the children. The Hopi would say, "The man is the slave, the clan is on the mothers side." The women had a strong voice in tribal affairs. Since, in most tribes, the woman inherited the name, they decided the matter of adoption and the fate of captives. In many tribes the women were healers and herbalists, and medicine women shamans. In some tribes they were the High Chief or called Women Sachems, Rowainers, Rainbow Women, Sunksquaws, or Queens, depending which tribe they were a part of. Succession to chief was usually a male on the mother's side. When a chief died or was ejected, the woman head of his clan would pick a new chief in consultation with other women council members. Out of all the women, the elder women were the ones in charge.

Operating Switchboard in 1925

The woman's position was summed up in the Iroquois confederacy by missionary Father Joseph Lafitau in 1724 when he said, "Nothing is more real however than the woman's superiority. It is they that maintain the tribe, the nobility of the blood, the genealogical tree, and the order of generations and conservation of the families. In them resides all the real authority; the lands, the fields, and all their harvest belong to them. They are the souls of the councils and the arbiters of peace and war. They hold the taxes and the public treasure. The slaves are entrusted to them, they arrange the marriages, the children are under their authority, and the order of succession is founded on their blood. The men, on the contrary, are entirely isolated and limited to themselves." Among the Lakota and Cheyennes, women usually ruled the camps. They owned the tepees and furnishings and many of the horses as well. The men did pretty much as the women wanted. Since the men were normally more conservative, the women acted as a spur. The women also usually outnumbered the men. A man's wives and sisters by blood provided for a close-knit family dominated by the oldest first-married wife. She was called "the sits-beside-him-wife," due to her place of honor in the lodge. The woman was never considered a slave. An eligible woman considered giving a gift to a prospective husband, who returned the favor, usually in horses to the woman's father. Marriage pacts were only concluded with the wholehearted consent of the bride. Feminine chastity was highly prized and absolutely required for most religious ceremonies.[11]

MEN: The man's role in Indian society was equally misunderstood by early Europeans. Men were responsible for hunting, defensive and aggressive warfare, manufacturing of weapons, and nearly all of society's wide political and

Buffalo Hunt   Lakota (Sioux) Chiefs on Horseback

religious operations. Observers who saw Indian men in their villages saw them "off work," although often they did help the women in the fields or in the construction of a lodge. When work took them away from the village, it was dangerous. They hunted on increasingly contested bison ranges and journeyed hundreds of miles to enemy encampments to steal horses and to win honors. The reciprocity of the gender roles is made clear by the hard facts of Indian demography: in most, if not all, Plains Indian societies in the mid–nineteenth century, there was far more women than men.

Men died in greater numbers and at earlier ages, victims of their dangerous occupations. Only in the late nineteenth century, when wars among the tribes and with the United States were curtailed, did the gender ratios equalize. By that time men and women alike were equally likely to die from poverty, alcohol, and the diseases that were brought to the Americas such as smallpox, tuberculosis, etc..[12]

A woman's highest calling is to lead a man to his soul so as to unite him with Source.

A man's highest calling is to protect woman so she is free to walk the earth unharmed.

~ Cherokee Proverb ~

COURTING: When dating, American Indians used specific types of rituals and customs throughout their history. Younger men and women were not allowed to choose their own partner or date around like modern day people do. Instead they spent time with people their father saw as acceptable and the father typically set up their relationships. The father looked for someone with power in the tribe or a strong warrior. The person may have met someone on their own, but their father had final say over the relationship. Some tribes, particularly the Lakota, used a process of gift giving by the male. As he courted the female he brought her gifts, though at times these gifts were meant for the whole family, or just the father. The father could accept the gifts and agree to the marriage and courtship without the daughter's knowledge. There was also a lack of private time for the young couple, as tradition required a chaperon. The belief was that girls must stay clean and pure, less they anger the Great Spirit.

American Indians tribes also used the court flute as a ritual. The man would play this flute near his potential love interest's home. She had the option of coming outside, which indicated her interest in him, or stay inside. If the woman didn't come out, the man left and was forced to find another woman. Other tribes used a system where the interested man left deer meat or another type of meat at the woman's house. If she was interested, she used the meat to cook for him and if not, she left the food sitting outside. The Cherokee used a ritual known as the Crane Dance during courtship. The unmarried women of the tribe wore clothes decorated with feathers and danced for the men. These dances usually lasted several days and gave the men of the tribe the chance to view the single women. The men chose their suitor during this dance and told their mothers, who then went about setting up the dating process.

Courting lasted anywhere from one to five years. A couple usually walked long distances talking not of love but of news and tribal affairs, with the man wrapping a blanket around the girl. Sometimes they exchanged rings made of metal or bone. Medicine men were consulted to provide love potions with which the youth might temp the girl. Spruce gum was a favorite. A white-tailed deer's tail, carried on the windward side of the girl's lodge so she could catch the scent, was another. Flutes at night played an influence on the girl, with her suitor staying up late at night to play for her. Courting the young girl was best when she performed her daily tasks of getting water or firewood. Once you found someone from another clan that you wanted to marry, there were rules you had to follow. A natural lesson to be learned from it is, that as in nature, it is the male who must prove his worth to the female and be patient in courting. First, you had to ask a family member if this was a good decision. You might have to hunt through several family members before you found someone who agreed with you that yes, this would be a good decision. If you could not find someone to agree with you, then you could not marry that person. Second, in some tribes you had to ask the chief of the women's village to determine if your marriage would be a good one. It was then the proposal was given to the woman through an intermediary, usually an older man, mutually respected by both of the families involved. In both Lakota and Cherokee society, marriages were often arranged by the parents and the formal request for a bride was made by presenting gifts to the bride's parents, who made the decision to accept or reject the marriage proposal. The bride price was usually food, blankets, fine clothing, and later horses.[13]

MARRIAGE: Women were well respected in Lakota culture. History has depicted Indians as savages because some men had plural marriages. However, the truth is that men had many wives because there were women that needed to be taken care of. The way Lakota society was structured demanded that everyone should be taken care of. Men depended on women, and women depended on men for survival. The women usually outnumbered the men about 2 to 1, due to the loss of men in the Indian tribes being killed in battles with adversaries and in the process of providing food by hunting. In many of the Indian tribes, if a man died in the hunt or war, his brother could marry the widow and take the children. This meant there were more women than men. Polygamy was common except for the Pueblo tribes. Few tribal men had more than four wives and the usual number was two. Multiple wives consisted most of the time as sisters. Having more wives meant that the work could be shared and everyone could be looked after properly. Young men married at twenty-five, as soon as they distinguished themselves in war. Girls married most of the time at puberty or after her first menstruation. An older woman would come and instruct her in her responsibilities of womanhood. A young girl at puberty had her whole body painted red by her grandmother. Naked and covered with a buffalo robe, she stood over a low smudge fire made from sage and juniper needles, letting the purifying smoke bathe her painted body. She stayed in a separate lodge for four days during which she ate no meat.

Seminole Wedding   Navajo Wedding

Some wedding ceremonies are informal, while others are quite formal, as they followed certain rituals of their tribal marriage. When they were not small and informal they were solemnized with feasts and merrymaking. Brides usually wear a red garment, instead of white, to their ceremony, which is often passed down through generations. But ceremonial clothing can differ from tribe to tribe. For example, in a Cherokee wedding the bride wears all white garb, consisting of a white dress and moccasins. The dress is made from pieces of cloth that tribe women tear into squares or rectangles. Cherokee grooms wear black pants, moccasins, and a reddish-orange shirt adorned with ribbons. In some tribes water is used as a symbol of purification and cleansing. The bride and groom have a ceremonial washing of hands to wash away past evils and memories of past loves. In the tribes of Northern California including the Klamath, Modoc, Yurok etc., the bride's dress may be woven in symbolic colors: white for the east, blue for the south, yellow (orange) for the

Quanah Parker, Comanche Chief with three wives, 1890

west, and black for the north. Turquoise and silver jewelry are worn by both the bride and groom in addition to a silver concho belt. Jewelry is considered a shield against evils, including hunger, poverty and bad luck. The Pueblo bride wore a cotton garment tied above the right shoulder and secured with a belt around the waist. Once married there was no set rule on where the couple should live, although most of the tribes were matrilocal, meaning the newlyweds would live in or near the wife's parents. In the marriage, both the woman and man are considered equal. This shocked the early Christian missionaries. The children of their marriages were raised by the mother's extended matrilineal clan. The female offspring of the mother remain living in (or near) the mother's house, thereby forming large clan-families typically consisting of three or four generations living in the same place. In-Law rules protected everyone from friction or disharmony. Modesty prevailed. A man might strip down to his breech clout for sleep or battle. But a woman stayed covered from shoulder to shin, except for her morning bath with other women in the river.[14]

FAMILY LIFE: The goal of the American Indian family and their parental support, within the context of the American Indian family, was to foster interdependence within the family. The

Seminoles Family, 2004   American Indian Family, 1899

entire American Indian family served as teachers in the development of its children. With the coming of the Europeans, an opposite contrasting affect of independence changed the American Indian family's lives from interdependence to being independent of ones' family. American Indian men have a harder time finding their place in contemporary society. The status of the Indian male has not risen anywhere near that of the Indian female. It is much harder for men to find employment that has the opportunity for career advancement.

Families slept in one room and sex education was a natural process, rather than being a secret or shameful thing. Disciplining the children was mild. Securing obedience was accomplished by frightening him or splashing water on him. Ridicule was often the best determent to misbehavior. Beating or slapping the child was rare. The Indians thought white parents treated their children as enemies. In adult life crime was rare. Since most property was communally owned, theft was almost unknown. Stealing horses from an enemy tribe was honorable, but stealing from their own people was unthinkable. Murder was seldom committed. If you were found guilty of murder the tribe could banish you for four years or a lifetime, according to the circumstances. Most tribes recognized these four virtues: Generosity, Bravery, Moral Integrity and Fortitude. These were the four sins recognized as unpardonable: (1) To permit anyone to go hungry, (2) To lose ones' eldest son in battle, (3) to permit the baby of a dead mother to cry from hunger, and (4) To return alone from war after one's comrades have been slain. [15]

HOMOSEXUALITY American Indians have often held gay and transgender, feminine males, and masculine females in high respect. The most common term to define such persons today is to refer to them as "two-spirit" people; embodying the spirits of both man and female. In American Indian cultures people did not

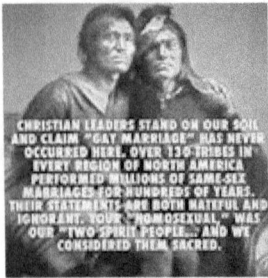

Two Spirit – Native American

Zuni - Wha'wa   Crow - Sharmen

make this an either/or situation. They viewed gender (and sexuality) as a continuum.

In the past, feminine males were sometimes referred to as "berdache" by early French explorers in North America, who adapted a Persian word, "bardaj," meaning an intimate male friend. Because these androgynous males were commonly married to a masculine man, or had sex with men, and the masculine females had feminine women as wives, the term berdache had a clear homosexual connotation. Both the Spanish settlers in Latin America and the English colonists in North America condemned them as "sodomites."

  Rather than emphasizing the homosexuality of these persons, however, many Native Americans focused on their spiritual gifts. American Indian traditionalists, even today, tend to see a person's basic character as a reflection of their spirit. Since everything that exists is thought to come from the spirit world, androgynous or transgender persons are seen as doubly blessed, having both the spirit of a man and the spirit of a woman. Thus, they are honored for having two spirits, and are seen as more spiritually gifted than the typical masculine male or feminine female. American Indians, rather than stigmatizing such persons, often looked to them as religious leaders and teachers. Quite similar religious traditions existed among the native peoples of Siberia and many parts of Central and Southeast Asia. They were often considered to be hard workers and artistically gifted and of great value to their extended families and community. Among some groups, such as the Navajo, a family was believed to be economically benefited by having a "nadleh" (literally translated as "one who is transformed") or androgynous person as a relative. Two-spirit persons assisted their siblings' children and took care of elderly relatives, and often served as adoptive parents for homeless children. A feminine male who preferred to do woman's work (gathering wild plants or farming domestic plants) was logically expected to marry a masculine male who did man's work (hunting and warfare). Because a family needed both plant foods and meat, a masculine female hunter, in turn, usually married a feminine female, to provide these complementary gender roles for economic survival. The gender-conforming spouse of two-spirit people did not see themselves as "homosexual" or as anything other than "normal."[16]

BOARDING SCHOOLS: Before and After

What happened to the power of men and women as well as the entire American Indian society and way of life? It was slowly wilted away by the Europeans. Then both the United States and Canada passed laws forcing the removal of Indian children to various religious schools to be brainwashed and beaten if they spoke their native language. The forced removal of Indian children from their families of origin by Bureau of Indian Affairs agents, and later missionaries acting on behalf of the government, was the single most damaging action taken against American Indian families.

Boarding schools were initially established in the late nineteenth century and continued to exist throughout the mid- to late 1960s. These schools were meant to educate American Indian children in the European-American tradition. The government's strategy was to remove American Indian children from their families of origin and place them in boarding schools, sometimes hundreds of miles away from their families and communities, with the goal of breaking up the traditional family, as well as to end their cultural way of life and religious practices.

In Canada these government run schools were also designed to "kill the Indian in the child" by separating them from their culture, language and their families. The children were also subjected to systematic abuse. An estimated 150,000 First Nation, Métis and Inuit youth were forced to attend these institutions between 1870 and 1996, when the last residential school closed.

Carlisle Indian School

* Established in 1879, the Carlisle Indian School was one of the first boarding schools for Native Americans.

* The students were forbidden to practice their religion or speak their language.

Before and after postcards were sold by the school to show off their "progress."

American Cultural Terrorism
Sexual Trauma: One Legacy of the Boarding School Era
Terrorists: Federal Government, Priests and Nuns

If the children were not around for the parents to teach cultural ways, then slowly, over time, the government would achieve its goal of exterminating American Indian culture and traditional family life and replace it with total assimilation to European-American society. Parents had sporadic or virtually no contact with their children while they were in the boarding schools. The end result was loss of family with parents suffering from unresolved grief and loss, high incidence of mental health problems and alcoholism, children who grew up not knowing their culture or how to parent when they became adults, identity struggles, generational transmission of the ramifications of boarding school experiences from fear or shame about identifying as an American Indian, and an inability to be good parents to their children through healthy and nurturing relationships.

RITUALS AND CEREMONIES:
Ceremony and rituals have long played a vital and essential role in American Indian culture. Although American Indians' spirituality in their ceremonies and rituals were often referred to as "religion," most did not consider it in the way Christians do. However, it was labeled as such by American writers, soldiers, and settlers, who did so perhaps because they didn't know how to otherwise describe the rituals and ceremonies. The American Indians, themselves, believed that their rituals and practices formed an integral part of their very being. Like other aboriginal peoples around the world, their beliefs were heavily influenced by their methods of acquiring food from hunting to agriculture. They also embraced ceremonies and rituals that provided power to conquer the difficulties of life, as wells as events and milestones such as puberty, marriage, and death. Over the years, practices and ceremonies changed with the tribes' needs. From tribe to tribe these rituals exhibited a great deal of diversity, largely due to the

Hoop Dance

relative isolation of various cultures that were spread out across the North American continent for thousands of years.

However, most tribes were closely connected to the land and the supernatural, addressing an ever-present invisible, universal force.

White Mountain Apache Rain Dance

The arrival of European settlers marked a major change in American Indian culture. Some of the first Europeans that the Indians would meet were often missionaries who looked upon Native American spiritual practices as worthless superstition inspired by the Christian devil. These early missionaries then determined to convert the Indians to Christianity. As more and more Europeans flooded North America, US and Canadian governments instituted policies to force Natives onto reservations and to encourage them to become assimilated into the majority culture. This also changed their spiritual traditions. For example in 1882, the U.S. Federal Government began to work towards banning American Indian Religious Rights, which impacted their ceremonies. At that time, U.S. Interior Secretary Henry M. Teller ordered an end to all "heathenish dances and ceremonies" on reservations due to their "great hindrance to civilization." This was further supported the following year by Hiram Price, Commissioner of Indian Affairs, when his 1883 report stated: "...there is no good reason why an Indian should be permitted to indulge in practices which are alike repugnant to

AMERICAN INDIAN SHAWL DANCE

common decency and morality; and the preservation of good order on the reservations demands that some active measures should be taken to discourage and, if possible, put a stop to the demoralizing influence of heathenish rites."

Perhaps the best known of these forms of suppression of American Indian religion is the Ghost Dance, which swept over a large part of the continent during the last decade of the 19th century.

In the past there were numerous Indian prophets of far reaching influence. One of them was Tenskwatawa, the famous brother of Tecumseh; another was the seer Smohalla of the Pacific coast; and even among the Eskimo such prophets have been known, particularly in Greenland. Sadly, once these movements became popular they were met with deadly force by the European settlers. A more recent attempt to suppress the American Indian traditions (as they attempted to regenerate their past lives and rid themselves of their invaders) led to the Massacre at Wounded Knee on

December 29, 1890, when the government attempted to stop the practice of the "Ghost Dance," Which was a far-reaching movement that prophesied a peaceful end to white American expansion and preached goals of clean living, an honest life, and cross-cultural cooperation by American Indians. When the Seventh U.S. Calvary was sent into the Lakota Sioux's Pine Ridge and Rosebud Reservations to stop the dance and arrest the participants, approximately 150 American Indian men, women, and children were killed, as well as their chief, Sitting Bull. Though some traditions were lost along the way, many others survived despite the ban, and various tribes continue to follow many spiritual traditions.

Some American Indians have been devout Christians for generations, and their practices today combine their traditional customs with Christian elements. Other tribes, particularly in the Southwest, have retained their aboriginal traditions, mostly intact. The Hopi Indians believe that the soul moves along a Sky Path, westwards, and that those who have lived a righteous life will travel with ease. However, those who haven't will encounter suffering on their journey. To ensure a safe journey, they wash their dead with natural yucca suds and dress them in traditional clothes. Prayer feathers are often tied around the forehead of the deceased, and they are buried with favorite possessions and feathered prayer sticks. Traditional foods and special herbs are served and placed at the graveside.

The Navajo perceived that living to an old age was a sign of a life well lived, thus ensuring that the soul would be born again. Alternatively, they felt that if a tribe member died of sudden illness, suicide or violence, a "Chindi, or destructive ghost, could cause trouble for the family of the deceased.

Afterlife rituals could last for several days, with careful thought given to foods and herbs chosen for the celebration—a reflection on how the deceased lived their life. Common herbs used by the Navajo included broom snake weed, soap weed, and Utah juniper.

Many tribes that had been converted to Catholicism also celebrated All Souls' Day each November 1st, which celebrates

Pueblo
Corn Dance

the dead. Many believe that on that day, the spirits return to visit family and friends. In preparation, various tribes would prepare food and decorate their homes with ears of corn as blessings for the dead. Also called the Green Corn Ceremonies, this is both a celebration and religious ceremony, primarily practiced by the peoples of the Eastern Woodlands and the Southeastern tribes, including the Creek, Cherokee, Seminole, Yuchi, Iroquois, and others. The ceremony typically occurs in the late summer and is tied to the ripening of the corn crops. Marked with dancing, feasting, fasting and religious observations, the ceremony usually lasts for three days. Activities varied from tribe to tribe, but the common thread is

Photo Bill Marder

Muskogee-Creek Ceremony

that the corn was not to be eaten until the Great Spirit has been given his proper thanks. Some tribes even believe they were made from corn by the Great Spirits.

The Green Corn Festival is also a religious renewal, with various religious ceremonies. During this time, some tribes hold council meetings where many of the previous years' minor problems or crimes are forgiven. Others signify the event as the time of year when youth come of age and babies are given their names.

Several tribes incorporate ball games and tournaments into the event. Cleansing and purifying activities often occur, including cleaning out homes, burning waste, and drinking emetics to purify the body. At the end of each day of the festival, feasts are held to celebrate the event and tribal members give thanks for the corn, rain, sun, and a good harvest. Green Corn Festivals are still practiced today by many different native peoples of the Southeastern Woodland Culture.[18]

Healing Ceremony

HEALING RITUALS:
Symbolic healing rituals and ceremonies were often held to bring participants into harmony with themselves, their tribe, or their environment. Ceremonies were used to help groups of people return to harmony; but large ceremonies were generally not used for individual healing. Some tribes, such as the Sioux and Navajo, used a medicine wheel, a sacred hoop, and would sing and dance in ceremonies that might last for days. Historic Indian traditions also used many plants and herbs as remedies or in spiritual celebrations, creating a connection with spirits and the after life. Some of these plants and herbs used

Sweat Lodge

in spiritual rituals included sage, bear berry, red cedar, sweet grass, tobacco, and many others. The healing process in American Indian medicine is much different than how most of us see it today. American Indian healing includes beliefs and practices that combine religion, spirituality, herbal medicine, and rituals that are used for both medical and emotional conditions. Traditional healers worked to make the individual "whole," believing that most illnesses stem from spiritual problems. In addition to herbal remedies, purifying and cleansing the body is also important and many tribes used sweat lodges for this purpose. The sweat lodge used for a purification ceremony is a hut, typically dome-shaped and made with natural materials, used by indigenous peoples of the Americas for ceremonial steam baths and prayer. In these darkened and heated enclosures, a sick individual might be given an herbal remedy, smoke or rub themselves with sacred plants, and a healer might use healing practices to drive away angry spirits and invoke the healing powers of others. Healing rituals might involve whole communities, where participants would sing, dance, and paint their bodies, sometimes use mind-altering substances to persuade the spirits to heal the sick person.[19]

PEYOTE WORSHIP: Some Southwest tribes have historically practiced peyote ceremonies, which were connected with the eating or drinking of tea made of peyote buttons, the dried fruit of a small cactus. Officially called Anhalonium or Laphophora, peyote is a small, spineless cactus with psychoactive alkaloids, particularly

mescaline. A standard cluster of the plant is shown, right. Native to the lower Rio Grande River and Mexico, the name "mescal" was wrongly applied to this fruit by many white observers. The ceremonies were held for specific reasons including healing, baptism, funerals, and other special occasions. Though many have the impression that peyote was smoked, this was not the case, as the peyote button will not burn. Instead, the buttons, either fresh or dried, were eaten or ground into a powder and drank in a tea.

Rites for these ceremonies would generally begin in the evening and continue until the following dawn and were restricted by some tribes only to men. Like other Indian ceremonies, a fire and incense were also used to cleanse the mind and body. The ceremony also utilized bird feathers, which represented their power—preferably those from predator birds, which were strong and thought to protect the worshiper. The ceremonies were guided by healers, also known as road men, as they were thought to guide a person's journey through life. Most often, small drums and rattles were also utilized. The experience is said to be almost identical to taking lysergic acid dyethylamide, better known as LSD. Called the "sacred medicine," peyote ceremonies are still practiced today by various tribes that believe that it counters the craving for alcohol, heals and teaches righteousness, and is useful in combating spiritual, physical, and other social ills. Concerned about the drug's psychoactive effects between the 1880's and 1930's, U.S. authorities attempted to ban Native American religious rituals involving peyote, including the Ghost Dance. Today, the Native American Church is one among several religious organizations allowed an exemption from the DEA to use peyote as part of its religious practice. In some states in the U.S., medical marijuana (cannabis) has been legalized as an antioxidant, and used in the treatment of diseases such as Alzheimer's, Parkinson's, HIV, etc.

According to scientific studies in 2015, cannabis is around 114 times less deadly than alcohol and was the only drug out of those examined to pose a low risk of death. [20]

VISION QUESTS:
Numerous Native American tribes practiced the rite of vision quests, which was often taken by older children before puberty to "find themselves" and their life's direction. How the rite was taken, its length and intensity, and at what age varied from tribe to tribe. In most cases the vision quest was a "supernatural" experience in which the individual seeks to interact with a guardian spirit, usually an animal, to obtain advice or protection. Much preparation was often taken before the vision quest was undertaken in order to determine the sincerity and commitment of the person. Sometimes the quest required the individual to go alone into the wilderness for several days, in order to become attuned to the spirit world. Other tribes required the individual to take a long walk, or were confined to a small room. Often the individual was required to fast prior to the quest, and was not allowed to sleep. During this period of sensory deprivation, the individual was to search for a guardian spirit's presence or a sign that would be given to them. Once the presence or sign was "seen" and the individual had realized his/her direction in life, they would return to the tribe to pursue their life's journey. [21]

MYTHOLOGY & SACRED CONCEPTS: The mythologies of the American Indians and the indigenous peoples of North America comprise many bodies of traditional narratives associated with religion from a mythological perspective.

Indigenous North American belief systems include many sacred narratives. Such spiritual stories are deeply based in Nature and are rich with the symbolism of seasons, weather, plants, animals, earth, water, sky and fire. Animal spirits in particular were very powerful and it was necessary to thank them and placate them if you wanted to make a meal of them. The principle of an all-embracing, universal and omniscient Great Spirit, a connection to the Earth, diverse creation narratives and collective memories of ancient ancestors are common. Traditional worship practices are often a part of tribal gatherings with dance, rhythm, songs and trance. The whole concept of the mythology of each tribe depends to a great extent on their religious concepts and activities. The mythologies are highly specialized in different parts of North and South America. Although a large number of myths are the common property of many American tribes, the general view of the world appears to be quite distinct in various parts of the continent. However, taking into consideration the continent of America as a whole, we find that an explanation of the world according to the American Indians is psychologically quite different from the biblical revelations in the Judaic religions. While a Great Spirit constitutes the basis of Indian theory, the tribes believe in multiple deities, which are surrounded by mythology. In accordance with their views of nature and spirit, they constantly appeal to these powers. They hear the Great Spirit in every wind; see him in every cloud; fear him in sounds, and adore him in every place that inspires awe. While cultures and customs varied among the tribes, they all believed that the universe was bound together by spirits of natural life, including animals, water, plants, the sky, and the Earth itself. Native American culture struggled to survive after the white man invaded their lives. Living through forced moves, war, starvation, diseases, and assimilation, these strong and spiritual people managed to keep their many legends and stories alive. Passed down through the generations, these many tales speak of timeless messages of peace, life, death, and harmony with nature.

The sacred beliefs of many tribes are largely expressed in sayings and narratives having some resemblance to the legends of European peoples. There are available large collections of these tales and myths from the Blackfoot, Crow, Nez Perce, Assiniboine, Gros Ventre, Arapaho, Arikara, Pawnee, Omaha, Northern Shoshone, and others. In these, much interesting information can be found. Though each tribe has its own beliefs and sacred myths, many have much in common. A deluge or flood myth is almost universal in the Plains tribes as with the Woodland Indians. Almost everywhere it takes the form of having the submerged earth restored by a more or less human being who sends down a diving bird or animal to obtain a little mud or sand. Other tales with common threads are the Twin-Heroes, The Woman Who Married a Star and Bore a Hero, and The Woman Who Married a Dog." A star-born hero is found in myths of the Crow, Pawnee, Dakota, Arapaho, Kiowa, Gros Ventre, and Blackfoot. Indian mythologies often contain large groups of tales reciting the adventures of a distinguished mythical hero with supernatural attributes who transforms, and in some instances creates, the world; who rights great wrongs and corrects great evils, yet who often stoops to trivial and vulgar pranks. Among the Blackfoot, for instance, he appears under the name of Napiw, also called "Old Man." He is distinctly human in form and name. The Gros Ventre, Cheyenne, Arapaho, Hidatsa, and Mandan seem to have a similar character in their mythology.

The "Old Man" also appears in the mythologies of adjoining culture areas, such as the area between the Plains and the Pacific Ocean. Some tales appear similar, but are attributed to an animal character with the name and attributes of a coyote. Under this name he appears among the Crow, Nez Perce, and Shoshone, on the western fringe of the Plains, but rarely among the Pawnee, Arikara, and Dakota, and practically never among the tribes designating him as human. Among the Assiniboine, Dakota, and Omaha, hero is presented as a spider-like character called Unktomi. In addition to heroes, many animal tales are to be found which often explain the structural peculiarities of animals as due to some accident. For example, the Blackfoot trickster, while in a rage, tried to pull the lynx asunder, causing it to have a long body and awkward legs. In other cases, the tales narrate an anecdote about the origin of life itself. In some tales, the ending includes how some aspect of life was "ordered to be," explaining a natural phenomena or mythical belief. There are also tales in which supernatural beings appear in the form of well-known animals and assist or grant favors to humans. In the mythology of the Plains tribes, the buffalo is a favorite character and is seldom encountered in the mythology from other areas. The bear, beaver, elk, eagle, owl, and snake are also frequently referred to, but occur in the myths of Woodland and other tribes. Of imaginary creatures the most conspicuous are the water monster and the thunderbird. The former is usually an immense horned serpent that stays under water and fears the thunder. The thunderbird is an eagle-like being that causes thunder. Migration legends and those accounting for the origins and forms of tribal beliefs and institutions make up a large portion of the mythology, formulating a concept of the religion and philosophy of various groups. In the Eskimo area, the mythology is characterized by an abundance of purely human hero-tales, and a very small number of traditions account for the origin of animals, and these are largely in a human setting. The North Pacific Coast area is characterized by a large cycle of transformer myths in which the origin of many of the arts of man is accounted for, as well as the peculiarities of many animals—

the whole forming a very disconnected, diverse mass of traditions.

Allied to these appear the traditions of the Western plateau and of the Mackenzie basin area, a region in which animal tales abound, many accounting for the present conditions of the world, the whole being very disconnected and contradictory. In the Californian area the mythologies are characterized by a stronger emphasis on creation by will power than is found in most other parts of the American continent. The principal characteristic of the mythologies of the area of the Great Plains, the eastern woodlands, and the arid Southwest, is the tendency to systematization of the myths under the influence of a highly developed ritual. This tendency is more sharply defined in the south than in the north and northeast, and has perhaps progressed further than anywhere else among the Pueblos, to whom the origin of the clans and societies seems to give the keynote of mythological concepts; and among the Pawnee, whose contemplation of the stars seems to have given them the principal tone to their mythology.

The religious concepts of the Indians deal largely with the relation of the individual to magical powers, and are specialized in accordance with their general mythological concepts, which determine largely the degree to which the powers are personified as animals, spirits, or deities. Social taboos are also practiced—an example of which includes never touching or even seeing the contents of sacred bundles. Other rules of conduct are not "taboos," but rather standards of behavior intended to retain the good will of the food animals and show them respect. The first game animals obtained at the beginning of the hunting season are always treated with particular care. The complicated customs relating to buffalo hunting, and the salmon ceremonials of the northwest Indians, as well as the whale ceremonials of the Eskimo, are a few examples. Dogs are not allowed to gnaw the bones of food animals, because it was a sign of disrespect. Among humans, respectful behavior toward the elderly and decent conduct are also counted among such required acts.

Rules of conduct may also include the numerous customs of purification that are required to avoid the ill will of the powers. These, however, may better be considered as constituting one of the means of controlling magic power, which form a very large part of the religious observances. Not satisfied with the attempt to avoid the ill will of the powers, the people also try to make them subservient to their needs. This end might be attained in a variety of ways. Perhaps one of the most characteristic methods of gaining control over supernatural powers was the acquisition of one of them as a personal protector. Generally, this process is called the acquiring of a manito, and the most common method of acquiring it is for the young man, during the period of adolescence, to purify himself by fasting, bathing, and vomiting until his body is perfectly clean and acceptable to the supernatural beings. At the same time, the youth works himself by these means by dancing, and sometimes also by means of drugs, into a trance in which he has a vision of the guardian spirit which is to protect him throughout life.

These means of establishing communication with the spirit world were also practiced at other periods of life in dances, "ordeals," and other rituals. The magic power that is acquired at these times is thought to give special abilities such as successful hunting, strength as a warrior, skills for priests, or even power to acquire wealth, success in gambling, or the love of women. It is also believed that there were other means of acquiring magic power, particularly among those tribes where strong clan organizations prevailed. In such cases, the people believe that wonderful powers may be attained by inheritance. Other cases, as among the Arapaho and Blackfoot, it is believed that acquiring this power and the control over it, can be purchased.

Among the American Eskimo, it is thought that the power may be transmitted by teaching and by bodily contact with a person who controls such powers. Ordinarily, its possession is considered so sacred that it must not be divulged except in cases of extreme danger, but among other tribes it may be made known to the whole tribe. Symbolic actions were also used to show their beliefs, such as the setting-up of prayer-sticks, which are meant to convey man's wishes to the powers. Often these wishes are indicated by special attachments, expressing in symbolic or pictographic manner the thing wished for.

Still more potent means of influencing the powers are offerings and sacrifices. Human sacrifice has been practiced on a number of different occasions and in many different cultures. It was practiced by the Aztecs as well as other Mesoamerican civilizations like the Maya and the Zapote. The Aztecs in Mexico sacrificed people in their belief that human sacrifice was the highest level of offering through which you could repay your debt to the gods. In North America, human sacrifice was practiced at an infinitesimally smaller scale compared to the Aztecs.

The most common form of human sacrifice was the ritualized torture of captured enemies. However, many cases of torture, particularly of self-torture, were a means to show your faith. Other bloody sacrifices are rare but sometimes exist—such as the sacrifice of the dog among the Iroquois and, to a limited extent, the killing of game as a bloody sacrifice. On the other hand, sacrifices of tobacco smoke, corn, other food, small manufactured objects, and symbolic objects, are very common. These gifts may be offered to any of the supernatural powers with the intent of gaining their assistance and avoiding their enmity.

In the same way that incantations are related to prayer, certain acts and charms are related to offerings. The custom of performing certain acts are effective through their own potency. Such acts are the use of lucky objects intended to secure good fortune; or the peculiar treatment of animals, plants, and other objects in order to bring about a change of weather.

There was a belief that the supernatural powers, if offended, may punish an individual. Such punishment may consist in the removal of the offender, who may be killed by the members of the tribe, or milder forms of punishment. Confession is a means of appeasement found among the Athapascan, the Iroquois, and the Eskimo. Other forms of punishment are based largely on the idea of purification by fasting, bathing, and vomiting. Among the Plains Indians the vow to perform a ceremony, or another act agreeable to the powers, is considered an efficient means of gaining their good will or of atoning for past offenses. [22]

There is no death
Only a change of worlds
- Chief Seattle

DEATH: American Indians celebrated death, knowing that it was an end to life on Earth, but believing it to be the start of a new life in the Spirit World. Most tribes also believed that the journey might be long, so afterlife rituals were performed to ensure that the spirits would not continue to roam the earth. Various tribes honored the dead in several ways by giving them food, herbs, and gifts to ensure a safe journey to the afterlife. The Hopi Indians believe that the soul moves along a Sky path westwards and that those who have lived a righteous life will travel with ease. However, those who haven't, will encounter suffering on their journey. The Navajo perceived that living to an old age was a sign of a life well lived, thus ensuring that the soul would be born again. Many of the

American Indian tribes had a belief that life is a journey that made a circle, and they had many medicine wheels that they used for understanding their path. There were generally common beliefs about the four directions and the totem animals of these directions. [23]

AMERICAN INDIAN HERBAL REMEDIES: A tremendous change has occurred in the diet of the American Indian since they were forced onto reservations and fed a different type of diet than they were accustomed to—especially with the Southwest Indians, where alarming diabetes rates and high rates of obesity is now common. The food that they ate in the past was very healthy, and the meat was very lean. Once they were forced off of their land into reservations, the food they were given had a high fat content, and they were doing much less work which led to excessive obesity and diabetes. Traditional foods were much healthier, and this is what many tribes are prescribing to combat the diabetes problem. Realizing this problem, the Department of Agriculture is partnering with tribes along the North and South Dakota border. Here the DA is offering fresh produce vouchers that the elderly can use at local markets. Overall, American tribes are moving toward a unification and traditional ways to combat a modern disease by attempting to rebuild their self-esteem that had been lost due to the genocide that was thrust on them. In the past, American Indian medicine men developed a wheel very similar to the yin/yang of Asian medicine. The use of herbal remedies and other alternative forms of treatment was the cutting-edge medicine of their day, relying heavily on plants and their unique benefits.

Medicine wheel located in the Bighorn National Forest

When it comes to herbal remedies, many of us are familiar with the benefits of Machinate or purple cone flower as an antibiotic, willow bark as a pain killer, and aloe as a topical anesthetic and treatment for skin conditions. But that's common knowledge compared to the insights and treatments that American Indian medicine men discovered and used.

Island Smith, Black American Indian Herb and Root Doctor

It's interesting that many of these natural cures are still in use today, including beeswax and bee pollen, chamomile and others. It's a good demonstration of the benefit of wisdom developed over the centuries. It's hard to know how American Indians determined which plants might have medicinal properties, although trial and error was probably one approach. It's also thought that they observed sick animals eating certain plants and determined that those plants must have a certain property worth exploring. Since that time, scientific studies have verified the medicinal value of many plants. In fact, common aspirin is derived from salicin, a chemical in the inner bark of willow trees that was used in ancient times for fever and pain. American Indian herbal remedies have been used to cure common illnesses and treat various health conditions. Without access to doctors or hospitals, Native Americans relied on the many plants that grew around their homes. Much of this knowledge has been forgotten; however there are those who are trying to document the remaining recipes. Many of the common natural medicines that are found in your local health food store are, or once were, American Indian remedies. Many of those herbs that the American Indian used were given to early settlers for their own maladies. These herbs have been used for generations, and many were in common medical use before conventional medications were developed. American Indians did not have some of the options for capsules and tinctures that we have. More than likely, most of their herbal remedies would have been made into teas. In many cases modern forms of these herbs serve the same purpose and work as well as the tea. These medicines were usually administered via teas or pastes that were either ingested or applied externally. Sometimes the plants were eaten as food or added to food or water. On occasion, a salve or poultice was applied to open wounds.[24]

QUOTES OF WISDOM

"This war did not spring up on our land, this war was brought upon us by the children of the Great Father who came to take our land without a price, and who, in our land, do a great many evil things... This war has come from robbery—from the stealing of our land." —**Spotted Tail**

"Being Indian is an attitude, a state of mind, a way of being in harmony with all things and all beings. It is allowing the heart to be the distributor of energy on this planet; to allow feelings and sensitivities to determine where energy goes; bringing aliveness up from the Earth and from the Sky, putting it in and giving it out from the heart." —**Brooke Medicine Eagle**

"The American Indian is of the soil, whether it be the region of forests, plains, pueblos, or mesas. He fits into the landscape, for the hand that fashioned the continent also fashioned the man for his surroundings. He once grew as naturally as the wild sunflowers, he belongs just as the buffalo belonged...." —**Luther Standing Bear, Oglala Sioux Chief**

"It was supposed that lost spirits were roving about everywhere in the invisible air, waiting for children to find them if they searched long and patiently enough...[The spirit] sang its spiritual song for the child to memorize and use when calling upon the spirit guardian as an adult." —**Mourning Dove (Christine Quintasket), Salish**

"We, the great mass of the people think only of the love we have for our land, we do love the land where we were brought up. We will never let our hold to this land go, to let it go it will be like throwing away (our) mother that gave (us) birth." —**Letter from Aitooweyah to John Ross, Principal Chief of the Cherokee**

"When a white army battles Indians and wins, it is called a great victory, but if they lose it is called a massacre." —**Chiksika, Shawnee**

"If you talk to the animals they will talk with you and you will know each other. If you do not talk to them you will not know them and what you do not know, you will fear. What one fears, one destroys." —**Chief Dan George, Tsleil-Waututh Nation, British Columbia, Canada**

"We are now about to take our leave and kind farewell to our native land, the country the Great Spirit gave our Fathers, we are on the eve of leaving that country that gave us birth, it is with sorrow we are forced by the white man to quit the scenes of our childhood... we bid farewell to it and all we hold dear."—**Charles Hicks, Tsalagi (Cherokee) Vice Chief speaking of the Trail of Tears, November 4, 1838**

"The land is sacred. These words are at the core of your being. The land is our mother, the rivers our blood. Take our land away and we die. That is, the Indian in us dies."—**Mary Brave Bird, Lakota**

"Once I was in Victoria, and I saw a very large house. They told me it was a bank and that the white men place their money there to be taken care of, and that by and by they got it back with interest. We are Indians and we have no such bank; but when we have plenty of money or blankets, we give them away to other chiefs and people, and by and by they return them with interest, and our hearts feel good. Our way of giving is our bank." —**Chief Maquinna, Nootka**

"We must protect the forests for our children, grandchildren and children yet to be born. We must protect the forests for those who can't speak for themselves such as the birds, animals, fish and trees." — **Qwatsinas (Hereditary Chief Edward Moody), Nuxalk Nation**

"Brother, you say there is but one way to worship and serve the Great Spirit. If there is but one religion, why do you white people differ so much about it? Why not all agree, as you can all read the Book?" — **Sogoyewapha, "Red Jacket," Seneca**

"Everything on the earth has a purpose, every disease an herb to cure it, and every person a mission. This is the Indian theory of existence." — **Mourning Dove [Christine Quintasket] (1888-1936), Salish**

"Upon suffering beyond suffering: the Red Nation shall rise again and it shall be a blessing for a sick world. A world filled with broken promises, selfishness and separations. A world longing for light again. I see a time of Seven Generations when all the colors of mankind will gather under the Sacred Tree of Life and the whole Earth will become one circle again. In that day, there will be those among the Lakota who will carry knowledge and understanding of unity among all living things and the young white ones will come to those of my people and ask for this wisdom. I salute the light within your eyes where the whole Universe dwells. For when you are at that center within you and I am that place within me, we shall be one." —**Crazy Horse, Oglala Sioux Chief (This statement was taken from Crazy Horse as he sat smoking the Sacred Pipe with Sitting Bull for the last time, four days before he was assassinated.)**

"A very great vision is needed and the man who has it must follow it as the eagle seeks the deepest blue of the sky." —**Crazy Horse, Sioux Chief**

"Whenever the white man treats the Indian as they treat each other, then we will have no more wars. We shall all be alike—brothers of one father and one another, with one sky above us and one country around us, and one government for all." —**Chief Joseph, Nez Perce**

"I am a red man. If the Great Spirit had desired me to be a white man he would have made me so in the first place. He put in your heart certain wishes and plans, in my heart he put other and different desires. Each man is good in his sight. It is not necessary for Eagles to be Crows. We are poor... but we are free. No white man controls our footsteps. If we must die...we die defending our rights." —**Sitting Bull, Hunkpapa Sioux**

"I have heard you intend to settle us on a reservation near the mountains. I don't want to settle. I love to roam over the prairies. There I feel free and happy, but when we settle down we grow pale and die." —**Satanta, Kiowa Chief**

"If the white man wants to live in peace with the Indian, he can live in peace.... Treat all men alike. Give them all the same law. Give them all an even chance to live and grow. All men were made by the same Great Spirit Chief. They are all brothers. The Earth is the mother of all people, and all people should have equal rights upon it.... Let me be a free man, free to travel, free to stop, free to work, free to trade... where I choose my own teachers, free to follow the religion of my fathers, free to think and talk and act for myself, and I will obey every law, or submit to the penalty." —**Chief Joseph, Nez Perce**

"The Great Spirit is in all things. He is in the air we breathe. The Great Spirit is our Father, but the Earth is our Mother. She nourishes us.... That which we put into the ground she returns to us." —**Big Thunder (Bedagi), Wabanaki Algonquin**

"These were the words given to my great-grandfather by the Master of Life: 'At some time there shall come among you a stranger, speaking a language you do not understand. He will try to buy the land from you, but do not sell it; keep it for an inheritance to your children.'" —**Aseenewub, Red Lake Ojibwa**

"My son, you are now flesh of our flesh and bone of our bone. By the ceremony performed this day, every drop of white blood was washed from your veins; you were taken into the Shawnee Nation..." —**Black Fish, Shawnee, recalling 1778 adoption of Daniel Boone into the tribe**

"When I am too old and feeble to follow my sheep or cultivate my corn, I plan to sit in the house, carve Katichina dolls, and tell my nephews and nieces the story of my life.... Then I want to be buried in the Hopi way. Perhaps my boy will dress me in the costume of a Special Officer, place a few beads around my neck, put a paho and some sacred corn meal in my hand, and fasten inlaid turquoise to my ears. If he wishes to put me in a coffin, he may do even that, but he must leave the lid unlocked, place food near by, and set up a grave ladder so that I can climb out. I shall hasten to my dear ones, but I will return with good rains and dance as a Katcina in the plaza with my ancestors..." —**Don Talayesva (late 19th century), Hopi Sun Clan Chief**

"What is life? It is the flash of a firefly in the night. It is the breath of a buffalo in the wintertime. It is the little shadow which runs across the grass and loses itself in the sunset." —**Crowfoot, Blackfoot warrior and orator**

"I was born upon the prairie, where the wind blew free, and there was nothing to break the light of the sun. I was born where there were no enclosures, and where everything drew a free breath.... I know every stream and every wood between the Rio Grande and the Arkansas. I have hunted over that country. I lived like my fathers before me, and like them, I lived happily." —**Ten Bears [Parra-wa-samem] (late 19th century), Yamparethka Comanche Chief**

"I do not see a delegation for the Four Footed. I see no seat for the Eagles. We forget and we consider ourselves superior. But we are after all a mere part of Creation. And we must consider to understand where we are. And we stand somewhere between the mountain and the ant. Somewhere and only there, as part and parcel of the Creation. "—**in an address to the Non-Governmental Organizations of the United Nations, Geneva, Switzerland, 1977, Chief Oren Lyons, Oneida**

"A long time ago this land belonged to our fathers, but when I go up to the river I see camps of soldiers on its banks. These soldiers cut down my timber, they kill my buffalo and when I see that, my heart feels like bursting."—**Satanta, Kiowa Chief**

"Conversation was never begun at once, nor in a hurried manner. No one was quick with a question, no matter how important, and no one was pressed for an answer. A pause giving time for thought was the truly courteous way of beginning and conducting a conversation. Silence was meaningful with the Lakota, and his granting a space of silence to the speech-maker and his own moment of silence before talking was done in the practice of true politeness and regard for the rule that, "thought comes before speech." —**Luther Standing Bear, Oglala Sioux Chief**

"For an important marriage the chief decided, aided by his wife. He passed a pipe around the room so each could share a smoke in common. In this way families were publicly united to banish any past or future disagreements and thus stood as "one united." The chief then gave the couple an oration of his advice, pointing out the good characteristics of each, and then offered his congratulations to them for a happy future." —**Mourning Dove [Christine Quintasket], Salish**

"It's our stuff. We made it and we know best how to use it and care for it. And now we're going to get it back." —**John Pretty on Top, Crow**

"The old Indian teaching was that it is wrong to tear loose from its place on the earth anything that may be growing there. It may be cut off, but it should not be uprooted. The trees and the grass have spirits. Whatever one of such growth may be destroyed by some good Indian, his act is done in sadness and with a prayer for forgiveness because of his necessities..." —**Wooden Leg (late 19th century), Cheyenne**

"Children were encouraged to develop strict discipline and a high regard for sharing. When a girl picked her first berries and dug her first roots, they were given away to an elder so she would share her future success. When a child carried water for the home, an elder would give compliments, pretending to taste meat in water carried by a boy or berries in that of a girl. The child was encouraged not to be lazy and to grow straight like a sapling." —**Mourning Dove [Christine Quintasket] (1888-1936), Salish**

"Out of the Indian approach to life there came a great freedom, an intense and absorbing respect for life, enriching faith in a Supreme Power, and principles of truth, honesty, generosity, equity, and brotherhood as a guide to mundane relations." —**Luther Standing Bear, Oglala Sioux Chief**

"The Earth is the Mother of all people, and all people should have equal rights upon it. You might as well expect the river to run backward as that any man who was born a free man should be contented when penned up and denied liberty to go where he pleases."
—Chief Joseph, Nez Perce

"I was warmed by the sun, rocked by the winds and sheltered by the trees as other Indian babes. I can go everywhere with a good feeling."
—Geronimo [Goyathlay], Chiracahua Apache

"Grown men can learn from very little children, for the hearts of the little children are pure. Therefore, the Great Spirit may show to them many things which older people miss." **—Black Elk, Oglala Sioux Holy Man**

"When a child my mother taught me the legends of our people; taught me of the sun and sky, the moon and stars, the clouds and storms. She also taught me to kneel and pray to Usen for strength, health, wisdom, and protection. We never prayed against any person, but if we had aught against any individual, we ourselves took vengeance. We were taught that Usen does not care for the petty quarrels of men." —
Geronimo [Goyathlay], Chiracahua Apache

"I want my people to stay with me here. All the dead men will come to life again. Their spirits will come to their bodies again. We must wait here in the homes of our fathers and be ready to meet them in the bosom of our mother." **—Wovoka, Paiute**

"A wee child toddling in a wonder world, I prefer to their dogma my excursions into the natural gardens where the voice of the Great Spirit is heard in the twittering of birds, the rippling of mighty waters, and the sweet breathing of flowers. If this is Paganism, then at present, at least, I am a Pagan." **—Zitkala-Sa**

"I will follow the white man's trail. I will make him my friend, but I will not bend my back to his burdens. I will be cunning as a coyote. I will ask him to help me understand his ways, then I will prepare the way for my children, and their children. The Great Spirit has shown me—a day will come when they will outrun the white man in his own shoes." —**Many Horses**

"I am poor and naked, but I am the chief of the nation. We do not want riches but we do want to train our children right. Riches would do us no good. We could not take them with us to the other world. We do not want riches. We want peace and love." —**Chief Red Cloud (Makhipiya-Luta), Sioux Chief**

"I was hostile to the white man.... We preferred hunting to a life of idleness on our reservations. At times we did not get enough to eat and we were not allowed to hunt. All we wanted was peace and to be let alone. Soldiers came... in the winter… and destroyed our villages. Then Long Hair (Custer) came.... They said we massacred him, but he would have done the same to us. Our first impulse was to escape... but we were so hemmed in we had to fight. After that, I lived in peace but the government would not let me alone. I was not allowed to remain quiet. I was tired of fighting.... They tried to confine me… and a soldier ran his bayonet into me. I have spoken." —**Crazy Horse, Sioux Chief**

"A warrior who had more than he needed would make a feast. He went around and invited the old and needy.... The man who would thank the food—some worthy old medicine man or warrior—said: "...look to the old, they are worthy of old age; they have seen their days and proven themselves. With the help of the Great Spirit, they have attained a ripe old age. At this age the old can predict or give knowledge or wisdom, whatever it is; it is so. At the end is a cane. You and your family shall get to where the cane is." —**Black Elk, Oglala Sioux Holy Man**

"In 1868, men came out and brought papers. We could not read them and they did not tell us truly what was in them. We thought the treaty was to remove the forts and for us to cease from fighting. But they wanted to send us traders on the Missouri, but we wanted traders where we were. When I reached Washington, the Great Father explained to me that the interpreters had deceived me. All I want is right and just." —**Chief Red Cloud (Makhipiya-Luta) Sioux Chief, April, 1870**

"Will we let ourselves be destroyed in our turn without a struggle, give up our homes, our country bequeathed to us by the Great Spirit, the graves of our dead and everything that is dear and sacred to us? I know you will cry with me, 'Never! Never!'" —**Chief Tecumseh, Shawnee**

"I hope the Great Heavenly Father, who will look down upon us, will give all the tribes His blessing, that we may go forth in peace, and live in peace all our days, and that He will look down upon our children and finally lift us far above the earth; and that our Heavenly Father will look upon our children as His children, that all the tribes may be His children, and as we shake hands today upon this broad plain, we may forever live in peace." —**Chief Red Cloud (Makhipiya-Luta) Sioux Chief**

"Great Spirit, Great Spirit, my Grandfather, all over the earth the faces of living things are all alike.... Look upon these faces of children without number and with children in their arms, that they may face the winds and walk the good road to the day of the quiet. —**Black Elk, Oglala Sioux Holy Man**

"We know our lands have now become more valuable. The white people think we do not know their value; but we know that the land is everlasting, and the few goods we receive for it are soon worn out and gone." —**Canassatego**

"In the beginning of all things, wisdom and knowledge were with the animals, for Tirawa, the One Above, did not speak directly to man. He sent certain animals to tell men that he showed himself through the beast, and that from them, and from the stars and the sun and moon should man learn... all things tell of Tirawa." —**Eagle Chief (Letakos-Lesa), Pawnee**

"You ask me to plow the ground. Shall I take a knife and tear my mother's bosom? Then when I die she will not take me to her bosom to rest. —**Wovoka, Paiute**

"If today I had a young mind to direct, to start on the journey of life, and I was faced with the duty of choosing between the natural way of my forefathers and that of the... present way of civilization, I would, for its welfare, unhesitatingly set that child's feet in the path of my forefathers. I would raise him to be an Indian!" —**Tom Brown, Jr.,** *The Tracker*

"You have noticed that everything as Indian does is in a circle, and that is because the Power of the World always works in circles, and everything tries to be round.... The Sky is round, and I have heard that the earth is round like a ball, and so are all the stars. The wind, in its greatest power, whirls. Birds make their nest in circles, for theirs is the same religion as ours.... Even the seasons form a great circle in their changing, and always come back again to where they were. The life of a man is a circle from childhood to childhood, and so it is in everything where power moves." —**Black Elk, Oglala Sioux Holy Man**

"There is no death. Only a change of worlds." —**Chief Seattle [Sealth], Suquamish Chief**

"Our lands—as indigenous lands—are the place where most of the oil and gas, and a good portion of the uranium and coal comes from. The easiest answer for the future generations is to keep it in the ground. And we are thankful for Bernie Sanders for saying, 'Let's keep it in the ground.' Don't make a mess we can't clean up." Environmentalist and economist, on her support for Bernie Sanders, Feb 25, 2016. —**Winona LaDuke, Activist**

"I hope to be remembered as a fighter and as a patriot who never feared controversy—and not just for Indians. When I fight for my people's rights, when I stand up for our treaties, when I protest government lies and illegal seizures and unlawful acts, I defend all Americans, even the bigoted and misguided." —**Russell Means** (November 10, 1939 – October 22, 2012)

TWENTY-FIRST CENTURY INDIAN VOICES
"WE SHALL OVERCOME"

Following are just a few accounts of the brave foot warriors that have personally suffered for American Indian rights and causes. They tell us below, only part of their tribulations and heroism while attempting to make a change. There are **many, many more** still active and working to help their own Tiyospe (family) and others to change their ways of living in this modern technological world.

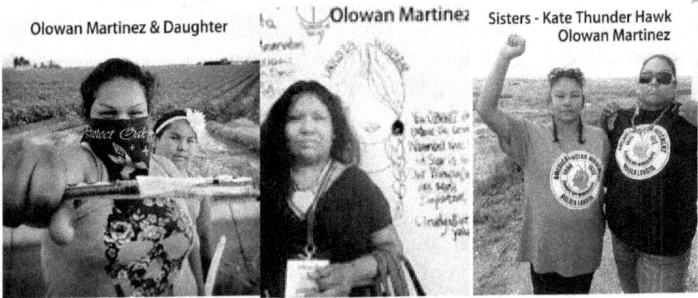

Olowan Martinez & Daughter

Olowan Martinez

Sisters - Kate Thunder Hawk
Olowan Martinez

Olowan Martinez (LiLii Red), Kate Thunder Hawk, & Clarence Rowland to Bill Marder, December, 2010:

In December of 2010, Olowan Martinez and Clarence Rowland began our journey towards reawakening the spirit of Liberation Day for our Oglala relatives, namely our youth whom are our future. It was a responsibility that we decided to take on in February of the same year when we encountered mass amounts of cross-generational confusion at the walk of Oglala Day and what it stood for to the Oglala people, amongst many other Indigenous people(s) across Turtle Island (North and South America). In that same regard we thought, "how could they carry

74

on the dream of our fallen warriors, with little to no understanding of the reasons why they did what they did?"

Olowan, coming from a social work background and myself, coming from a teaching background, were born into the struggle of the 70's by parents who stood and fought for the future of the Lakota and our grandchildren. It is for those very reasons that our parents made sure that we understood what it was they were fighting for. They planted a seed into our hearts and minds as children and simply put, we just never forgot. As we grew up and fine-tuned ourselves into the scheme of things as native women, we decided from the beginning that we were not in control of anything. We understood that our ancestors were the ones who were guiding us and making things happen at a rapid pace. We began our journey trekking across Native America to research and find an understanding that would benefit the future. Every time we would bring someone's name up that we heard of from the 70's, within minutes the phone would ring and there would be a connection for us to meet with them. Some days we would just look at one another and say, "Law of attraction for our ancestors are on our side" and boom, it would happen. All of a sudden we had t-shirts, a gym to feed in, transportation, food, fliers, printing money, a laptop, a printer, etc. Everything we needed was coming so rapidly that we had no choice but to embrace our ancestors, as they were truly the ones guiding us. We both know now more than ever that our ancestors want our relatives to exist rather than to just 'be.' In the beginning we were provided a vehicle from my mother, which, by the way, didn't have any heat.

Clarence Rowland and Family (Tiyospaye)
Remembrances of those who died too early in life

A few days in, and off we went on a mission to keep the flame going so that our 8th fire can be lit and our Lakota relatives will exist once again. Unbeknown to us, through the eyes of the old, we, ourselves, learned how to 'exist' once again. We also came to the conclusion that the Ozuye (warriors) from the 70's can never be replicated—only sought after through stories and gatherings.

On that same note, and through the understandings that grew from the events of the 70's, we understood that everything that we do as Lakota people we must do with prayer. So we drove to Sicangu (Rosebud) to offer tobacco to one of our Ozuye from that era, Uncle Crow Dog, so that he may come and pray on Liberation Day. We then drove to every community on the Pine Ridge Indian Reservation to distribute fliers; we went to Rapid City on several occasions to pick up supplies; all this in my mother's little Honda Accord with no heat. Sometimes we would be sitting on the side of the road for hours with our ring of red and a loaf of bread trying to keep warm with what little heat was coming out of the vents; all for our nation to exist once again.

We would just laugh and say, "Our ancestors are on our side."
One night we were parked at Pinky's store in Manderson on our
last leg of delivering fliers to our communities when I looked up
to see a semi fly by our little reservation road. Here we were
sitting there trying to keep warm like two little grandma's, each
wrapped in blankets, when I looked at Olowan and said, "Sis,
twelve years ago I drove through Scenic and came upon a road
block on the reservation line by one of our warriors from the
70's. He had tipi's set up and was stopping all semis from
entering our reservation because they were tearing up our roads.
Look! It didn't work. What are we doing wrong?" She said,
"Who was it, sis?" I said, "Dave C." She just looked off into the
iced-filled windshield and nodded her head. Later she told me
that she remembered so many of our warriors at that very
moment who made their journeys home with their battles
unfinished. She was deeply saddened, as was I, for both of us
thought of our parents; her mom and dad and my dad, who both
left with their battles unfinished as well. Ultimately, we
discovered so much about ourselves and what it means to be a
Lakota in modern times. After the many visits and many
research tactics, we found out that the American Indian
Movement didn't originate within the Oglala. It was a
"movement" that began soon after the Relocation Act of 1956,
which placed indigenous people out of their reservations and into
the cities. It was these groups of families who were outraged at
the atrocities that were bestowed upon indigenous people(s) of
Turtle Island that started the American Indian Movement. Of
these families, they had grandmas who wanted something done
so that America would never forget that there were still
indigenous people(s) here and we were still alive. Most
importantly, the struggle lives on. They came up with the name
American Indian Movement. Almost simultaneously a group of
elders here on the Pine Ridge Indian Reservation came together

and they called for AIM to come and help them. There were countless sufferings that were taken place during that time which included numerous murders within the Oglala people.

Many of the murders were by our own relatives. This is why sometimes you will hear people refer to these times as "AIM and GOON days." Yet, what we discovered with that was that it was another "divide and conquer" tactic to keep our relatives in oppression. At that moment we knew that we had to truly look through the eyes of the elders of those times in order to comprehend the reasons why they did what they did. We came up with this: when the elders here within the Oglala called AIM in to come and help, it was their last leg, their last chance, their last hope to save the future of their grandchildren—for they were watching Oglala's kill Oglala's. It was a sad, sad time. When AIM came in, countless members of our Oglala relatives joined the movement and that is why you will find people stating today, "I am a second generation AIM baby." These comments are being made today because these are the ones that are the seeds of our relatives who were very proud of the changes that took place within our communities after the 71-day standoff that took place in 1973. It was after this day that we didn't have to run with our pots of soup and duck and hide to have ceremony. It was after this day that our men wore long braids once again. It was after this day that Lakota names became more prominent. It was after this day that the elders seen a better tomorrow for their grandchildren. It was after this day that we began our journey towards the path to which the grandfathers and grandmothers on the other side intended us to live, collectively. It is because of this 71-day stand-off that you will see our relatives speak their language, attend ceremony, have naming ceremonies and go to sweat lodge today.

I was born in 1977, four years after the events that took place in 1973 and I was born with a Lakota name. If '73 didn't happen I could have been a Barbara Ann or a Sally Marie or something crazy like that. Yet, because I was born into the struggle, I came here Lakota and remain Lakota to this day. On February 27th, 2011 something beautiful happened; a flame was sparked and it was cross-generational. Through the four-directional spiritual walk and ride, the ones who will one day fill our moccasins were able to see the reasons why 1973 happened through the eyes of our elders. Through the spirit of our AIM song, the spirit of those who walked before us in 1973 was reawakened through the eyes of the future. Through prayer and belief, our peers were compelled to step up to the plate and find their warrior within so that our future may thrive. Through honor and courage we seen people come out and share about their loved ones. Through strength and willingness we were able to hear the anger within many of our relatives in the "homeland" because of what happened in 1973. Yet through it all we saw healing taking place within each generation that were present on this very good red day. It is because of these things that we are able to heal, able to come alive and most of all, able to levitate our elders' dream into the next generation(s) so that they may pick up the dream and carry it on for the next 40 years. Mitakuyapi (all my relatives), this event is living proof that 1973 didn't happen for nothing. On this day today in 2011 a spark took place from within; from those not yet born, all the way up to the elders. They all walked away feeling proud once again to be Lakota. The elders and ancestors on the other side are smiling for they know now that the Oglala will "exist" once again. All these things I speak of I want you to know that my sister Olowan and I had nothing to do with it. It was all of our ancestors who are on the other side dancing and singing our nation strong; we merely chose to embrace them and become the flexible stem of a plant so that they may be able to work through us to bring healing to our nation.

To our elders: Please forgive us for our hearts are pure, everything we did was in honor of you; your warriors who sparked our souls before we were even thought of in 1973. WE cherish you.

To our youth: Please understand that everything that we did was in your honor, for one day you will precede us in maintaining the flame from within. WE believe in you.

To our peers: We challenge you to come and help us next year. Hecetu We Ksto (that is the way it is); Mitakuye Oyasin (all my relatives). We believe in your warrior, and Pte San Win (White Buffalo Calf Woman).

Olowan Sara Martinez, **February 7, 2010**: I can only ask this: Don't give up. Not ever. Stay in this fight with me. Suffer with me. Grieve with me. Endure with me. Believe with me. Outlast with me. And one day, celebrate freedom with me. Hoka hey! In the Spirit of Crazy Horse, Leonard Peltier.

Sacheen Seitcham, January 30, 2016: Ahousat, BC, Canada.

Dear Young confused hurting and lashing out native women, I hear you and I feel you, I too know the rage and pain and fear your going through. Your life and body is not your own, your heart and mind hard-wired for pre-colonization goals and we are left with capitalism and Kardashians and Jersey Shore instead of coming of age ceremonies. I know how proud and shamed you are of being Indian and being a women and being different than society, being poor and feeling poorly cared for. It's hard to break a cycle and break away from the way white society and white media tells us is normal, and we want to hurt ourselves and our families because our hurt is so huge we can barely contain it in our own bodies and spirits. BUT you must be vigilant and be on guard because you are way too precious and too valuable to us to run away and disappear into a life on the streets and the clubs. You have a responsibility to yourselves and your tisopaye. We are missing, many Raped and Murdered Indigenous Women. It is a harsh and heart-breaking reality, so please, before your run away, or you choose the parties and the lifestyle of the poor and impoverished, remember in your heart and your soul that YOU ARE THE MISSING LINK! Remember your mothers are not perfect but we are here and we love you and we want you to succeed and to stay home and work it out! You can never get these years back, so even though it is hard and maybe one of the hardest things you will do, ask for help, and find a way to be healthy. You are power incarnate; you carry the blood of our ancestors and all the new generations yet to come in your womb. You are the light!—connected by our umbilicus to Mother Earth and our traditions, you are the result of hundreds of years of our women surviving and striving and sacrificing body, life and land so you could exist today, and without you our nations are weak! Embrace your strength as a warrior and a women, embrace your life and your culture, embrace your womb and your sisters and together we shall RISE! Native women rising are the most powerful, beautiful creatures to behold! With much love, Xhopakelxhit, your mother, your sister, your grandmother, your cousin, your aunty, and your friend.

Okichize Wiohitika Win (Autumn Two Bulls,) and daughter,

Daughter Okichize Wiohitika Win
Ta'teyatopa
dlowan win

Ta'te: February 16, 2015: In life we encounter many hardships, struggles, emotional breaks, heartbreaks, losses, battles, addictions, physical elements, but if we hold our prayer close to our hearts and believe in our power of prayer, we will get through all the obstacles of life. I'm always there for others, caring for and loving people no matter how hurt I am; how broken I may feel at times. I don't give up on loving myself because I have a lifetime to love the Creator and others. That's what this life is all about. If we don't love ourselves, we lose all focus of life and its good qualities. I was raised very strong in the Lakota traditional beliefs. In those teachings I was taught about balance and self-love. With that being said, I need to love myself a little more so that I don't lose focus on the important things in life—my prayer, my sacred journey through life. I overcame so much in this life that I truly honor myself for those things. I've been hurt and broken by others almost since the time of my existence, but I was given a very special gift and that is my Lakota way of life. And that way of life has brought me through the most difficult times in life. All the struggles and battles. I'm just expressing myself now, with much love. I hope some of the things I share might help somebody out there. Because I know when I'm going through things in life, there have been people who have helped me.

Margaux Simmons
Activist & Musician

Margaux Simmons: I am Cherokee/Shawnee/African American ancestry, a musician, music composer and a member of the Fire Lightning Tiospaye which owns the land where the victims of the 1890 massacre are buried, as is my mother. I was curator of the Museum at Wounded Knee, which stands on that sacred land, from 2007-2010. I went to the US State Department with Russell and Pearl Means, Phyllis Young and others to deliver the letter of independence and to establish the Republic of Lakotah in 2007. I was highly honored to have worked with Pearl, Phyllis and Russell—who worked tirelessly all of his life for the benefit of the Lakota People and all indigenous people. He was not afraid to say or do what was necessary to help people in need. When I came to Pine Ridge in 2006, my eyes were opened to the plight of my relatives who struggle daily against the shackles of colonialism and genocide in the forms of alcohol, drugs and extreme poverty. I could see that the trenches of colonialism were dug very deeply, however, in the way that domestic abuse had taken hold as a way of life. Lying, stealing and patriarchy were now accepted ways of living; ways that would not have been tolerated in traditional Lakota society. The invaders' genocidal tactics now work on their own and seem to be systemically ingrained in the tribal political system that's set up by the US government, just as it was in 1973, when AIM was called into Pine Ridge by the local people because of mistreatment by the members of the OST, the Oglala Sioux Tribal Council. Today, there is a mass movement by the young people and the women to take back the old ways: the way to our future is through our past. Through unity we all fight for sobriety, self-determination and sovereignty, the principles of AIM.

DRUGS: Meth: Mothers Against Meth Alliance (M.A.M.A),

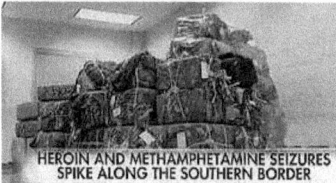

HEROIN AND METHAMPHETAMINE SEIZURES
SPIKE ALONG THE SOUTHERN BORDER

now worldwide, has been leading the fight against this epidemic let loose on American Indians and others. Methamphetamine is an extremely addictive stimulant. It was developed in Japan as a diet pill and when found to be addictive, was removed from the market. Methamphetamine was, however, used by Japanese troops during World War 2 and by Hitler's Storm Troopers. Hitler himself was addicted, receiving daily injections to the end of his life. The form of methamphetamine available in the 40s and 50s was not nearly as potent as the Ice form of the drug found now. The Ice form of methamphetamine is more potent and more addictive than the old "speed" from years ago. The Ice form of the drug can be smoked like crack cocaine. Methamphetamine is nearly impossible to stop.

"MY NAME IS METH" Written by a young American Indian girl who was in jail for drug charges, and was addicted to meth. She wrote this while in jail. As you will read, she fully grasped the horrors of the drug, as she tells in this simple, yet profound poem. She was released from jail but, true to her story, the drug owned her. They found her dead not long after, at age 14, with the needle still in her arm.

My Name Is "Meth"

I destroy homes, I tear families apart, take your children, and that's just the start.
I'm more costly than diamonds, more precious than gold,
The sorrow I bring is a sight to behold.
If you need me, remember I'm easily found,
I live all around you—in schools and in town.
I live with the rich; I live with the poor;
I live down the street and maybe next door.
I'm made in a lab, but not like you think,
I can be made under the kitchen sink,
In your child's closet, and even in the woods.
If this scares you to death, well it certainly should.

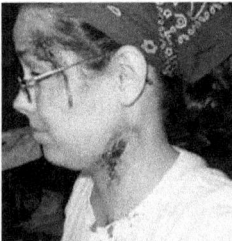

I have many names, but there's one you know best,
I'm sure you've heard of me, my name is crystal meth.
My power is awesome; try me, you'll see,
But if you do, you may never break free.
Just try me once and I might let you go,
But try me twice, and I'll own your soul.

When I possess you, you'll steal and you'll lie,
You do what you have to—just to get high.
The crimes you'll commit for my narcotic charms
Will be worth the pleasure you'll feel in your arms,
your lungs, your nose.
You'll lie to your mother; you'll steal from your dad,
When you see their tears, you should feel sad.
But you'll forget your morals and how you were raised,
I'll be your conscience, I'll teach you my ways.
I take kids from parents, and parents from kids,
I turn people from God, and separate friends.
I'll take everything from you, your looks and your pride,
I'll be with you always—right by your side.
You'll give up everything—your family, your home,
Your friends, your money, then you'll be alone.
I'll take and take, till you have nothing more to give,
When I'm finished with you, you'll be lucky to live.
If you try me be warned—this is no game,
If given the chance, I'll drive you insane.
I'll ravish your body, I'll control your mind,
I'll own you completely, your soul will be mine.
The nightmares I'll give you while lying in bed,
The voices you'll hear, from inside your head.
The sweats, the shakes, the visions you'll see,
I want you to know, these are all gifts from me.
But then it's too late, and you'll know in your heart,
That you are mine, and we shall not part.
You'll regret that you tried me, they always do,
But you came to me, not I to you.
You knew this would happen, many times you were told,
But you challenged my power, and chose to be bold.
You could have said "no," and just walked away,
If you could live that day over, now what would you say?

85

I'll be your master, you will be my slave,
I'll even go with you, when you go to your grave.
Now that you have met me, what will you do?
Will you try me or not? It's all up to you.
I can bring you more misery than words can tell,
Come take my hand, let me lead you to hell.

Ebony Tiger, a 17-year-old of the Yankton Sioux Tribe related her experiences on March, 2016 at a Meth Summit Tribal conference.

I am here to tell you how methamphetamine has affected my life. My mother is an addict, and has been for most of my life. I've lived with demons on my back for so long…. It's not easy living in the shadow of my mother's addiction… it takes a toll on my life… at one point, I became so depressed I didn't have the motivation to do anything. Every day was like living in a prison. I was left in the care of people I did not know… I never had a home. I never felt the love I saw being given to other children. Many bad incidents occurred between me and my mother because her addiction got the best of her. In 2014, one of these incidents ended very badly…

CHILDREN FOR SALE: A BROKEN SYSTEM: The Indian Child Welfare Act (ICWA) was enacted in 1978 due to the high removal rate of Indian children from their traditional homes and essentially from Indian culture as a whole. Before enactment as many as 25 to 35 percent of all Indian children were being removed from their Indian homes and placed in non-Indian homes. In some cases, the Bureau of Indian Affairs (BIA) paid the states to remove Indian children and to place them with non-Indian families and religious groups. Testimony in the House Committee for Interior and Insular Affairs showed that in some cases, the per capita rate of Indian children in foster care was nearly 16 times higher than the rate for non-Indians. Their parental and human rights have been violated for a great number of years, resulting in human trafficking of children in violation of our 13th amendment. One of the factors in this judgment was that, because of the differences in culture, what was in the best interest of a non-Indian child were not necessarily what was in the best interest of an Indian child, especially due to extended families and tribal relationships.

Across the United States, Indian parents have complained. States have not complied with the Indian Child Welfare Act when parents seek to get back their children. The system fights anyone challenging them, with parents facing seemingly never-ending rounds of requirements, paperwork and checklists that thwart their attempts to regain custody of their own children after they disappear into state custody.

In 2015 a federal judge ruled that a South Dakota state judge's five-minute hearing that remove Native American children from their homes violates the Indian Child Welfare Act. The Oglala Sioux and Rosebud Sioux tribes and two Sioux parents sued the presiding judge of South Dakota's 7th Circuit, the district attorney of Pennington County, the Secretary of the South Dakota Department of Social Services, and the person in charge of Social Services' Child Protection Services in Pennington County. U.S. District Judge Jeffrey Viken directed most of his judicial wrath at Pennington County Circuit Court Judge Jeff Davis, the presiding judge of South Dakota's 7th Circuit, by saying, "Judge Davis typically conducts hearings within 48 hours of an Indian child's removal from the parents' care. The hearings usually last less than five minutes. The removed Indian children often spend weeks or months in foster care away from their parents, Indian custodians and tribes." Davis also denies parents the chance to cross-examine the affidavit's signer or to present evidence. Each child placed makes the state about $62,000 in profit!

Children are often removed from the home with little or no effort to keep the family together, and without expert testimony about whether continued custody by the Indian parent or guardian is likely to physically or emotionally endanger the child. Viken wrote that he found that Davis' policies have allowed him to efficiently "rubber stamp" the removal of hundreds of Indian children. "It was noted," concluded Viken, "that Judge Davis and the other defendants failed to protect Indian parents' fundamental rights to a fair hearing. Indian children, parents and tribes deserve better."

This suffering must stop!

THE STOLEN ONES
Can anyone hear the children weep
Not out loud but in their sleep
Sounds like hurt
Held deep inside
Like they don't know what they all hide
Do they feel there's something wrong
That something's missing, something strong?
Family ties too far away
Brothers and sisters all here to stay
Hear! Hear the children weep
Not out loud, in their sleep
Something's wrong!
Nothing strong
Hear them, hear them, the children weep
My love, hope and strength to those families. [25]

This poem speaks of the suffering of families whose children are taken from them and those children who are forced to assimilate into a culture and system not of their own by governments not just here in North America, but also in the indigenous countries throughout the World.

There is an epidemic of suicides in both the USA and Canada, particularly with teenagers that have given up hope under the conditions they live under. In the USA, 425 children between the ages of 10 and 14 died by suicide in 2014 compared to 242 in 1999. Most of the deaths involved 13- and 14-year-olds. Suicides among young American Indians are double the national rate. The numbers are even higher because deaths overall in the American Indian communities are under-reported by as much as 30 percent.

INDIAN HEALTH SERVICE—Problems: (IHS) is an agency within the U.S. Department of Health and Human Services. A Senate committee meeting heard testimony February 12, 2016 on the Indian Health Service. In one reported incident it was stated that a patient drove 35 miles to the closest IHS facility and spent four hours there to get her medication. She drove all the way home and found that she had been administered the wrong medication. When she called and told them she had the wrong medication, they told her to flush it down the toilet rather than to return and exchange it. She stated that on multiple occasions the IHS has treated her as with extreme "negligence." Problems like this have been happening for decades and the fact that they're still happening today is unacceptable.

In 2013, Indian Health Service spending for patient health services was $2,849 a person, compared with $7,717 for health care spending nationally, according to a report from the National Congress of American Indians. The IHS is way underfunded despite the fact that American Indians typically have more serious health problems than the general public, including higher rates of diabetes, liver disease and unintentional injuries. Most of the patients are the poorest of the poor. IHS has specialty clinics, but the lack of funding and doctors has caused that system to fail.

The lack of funds is due to budget cuts from Washington and it keeps getting worse. The Area Offices of IHS take more of the funding, leaving a much less amount to Service Units on reservations and urban areas. IHS health care is very poor, and patients cannot be helped many times because IHS can't always provide the service for the patients' health issue. Most of the people employed in IHS have no management or business skill in the position they hold. If IHS doesn't provide the service for your health issue they will refer you out to another hospital, and that is where one is stuck with a bill.

In some states, American Indians with low incomes can sign up for expanded Medicaid. Exceptions are found in states like South Dakota, where a large number of Indians live. Lawmakers have not expanded Medicaid coverage to these low-income adults here, leaving thousands of people, most of them urban, poor American Indians, without health coverage. The health care system is inherently and systemically rooted in racism, as American Indians have sometimes been allowed to die in emergency rooms.

Shinnecock Indian Nation

BLACK INDIANS: Contact between Africans and American Indians date back to April 1502, when the first enslaved Africans arrived in Hispaniola and were mentioned in a report by Nicolas de Ovando, Governor of Hispaniola. Some Africans escaped inland from the colony of Santo Domingo, and joined with the American Indians to became the earliest Black Indians. The first slave rebellion occurred in Hispaniola in 1522, while the first on future

United States soil (North Carolina) occurred in 1526. Both rebellions were organized and executed by coalitions of Africans and Indians. Europeans feared these communities of escaped Africans, known as Maroons. Many blacks escaped slavery, as well as being captured in raids by the Indians—who then integrated them into their tribes and sometimes intermarried with them. This was especially true with the Cherokees, who sheltered and intermarried with many before they were forced to leave their land and homes to go on their "Trail of Tears" to Oklahoma. Black American Indians were well represented in the Trail of Tears.

This alliance occurred despite all efforts by the Whites to try to split them apart. By 1860, the Five Civilized Nations in the Indian Territory consisted of 18 percent African Americans. The Seminoles had appointed six Black Seminole members on its governing council. In 2006, the Cherokee Nation Supreme Court ruled that descendants of Freedmen, as well as of Intermarried Whites listed on the Dawes Rolls (where both groups were listed in separate categories), should be allowed to enroll in the Cherokee Nation. A cultural bond now exists between both of these groups, since each have been forced to live through their own genocide.

One important factor that came up was the problem of Black Indians, White Indians, Hispanic Indians, etc.—that for one reason or another were incorporated into the tribes, many over 100 years ago. They have been called half-breeds, mixed bloods, Metis (a mixture of French and Indian), etc. What part do they play in American Indian society? I discussed this fully in my book *Indians In The Americas.* Today the term "blood quantum" is used to describe the measurement of tribal blood one has, percentage-wise, and how much is required to be considered a full-blooded Indian. This began to get complicated without a recognized standard. Some tribes may require 50% to be admitted, while others acknowledge only $1/32^{nd}$ of their blood to become a tribal member, while other tribes require one to prove they are 100% full-blooded. In my opinion, living as an American Indian is not only about skin color or blood quantum. Many of the blood quantum Indians, in whatever percentage, have followed their tribal practices for many years, so have been integrated into the tribes. They follow the same teachings and philosophy of a full-blooded Indian—or maybe even more so.

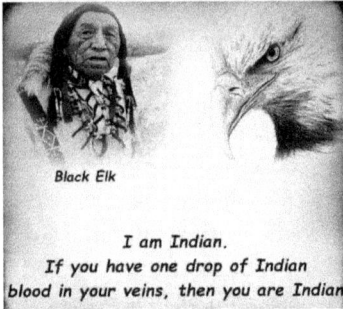

Black Elk

I am Indian.
If you have one drop of Indian blood in your veins, then you are Indian

The entire concept of a pure Indian or of a mixed-race, mixed-blood, hybrid, mud blood, half-breed, Métis etc., is all a fallacy of the mind created by white colonialism to establish a hierarchy of those at the top and subordinates below. What bothers me is the fact that ignorant people assume that once someone is considered mixed, that person is immediately stereotyped as being less of an individual. Instead, the individual should be recognized as neither Indian or White—but both. It is more important that the individual can feel connected to his tiyospaye (family,) to his tribe, and most of all, connected to the entire human race. We call it "Mitakuye Oyasin"(we are all related).

HISTORY OF AMERICAN INDIAN ACTIVISM

During the late 1960s and early 1970s, a new spirit of political militancy arose among the first Americans, just as it had among black Americans and women. No other group, however, faced problems more severe than Native Americans. Throughout the 1960s, American Indians were the nation's poorest minority group, more deprived than any other group, according to virtually every socio-economic measure. In 1970, the Indian unemployment rate was 10 times the national average, and 40 percent of the Native American population lived below the poverty line. In that year, Native American life expectancy was just 44 years, a third less than that of the average American. In one Apache town of 2,500 on the San Carlos reservation in Arizona, there were only 25 telephones, and most homes had outdoor toilets and relied on wood burning stoves for heat. Conditions on many of the nation's reservations were not unlike those found in underdeveloped areas of Latin America, Africa, and Asia. The death rate among Native Americans exceeded that of the total U.S. population by a third. Deaths caused by pneumonia, hepatitis, dysentery, strep throat, diabetes, tuberculosis, alcoholism, suicide, and homicide were 2 to 60 times higher than the entire U.S. population. Half a million Indian families lived in unsanitary, dilapidated dwellings; many in shanties, huts, or even abandoned automobiles. On the Navajo reservation in Arizona, roughly the size of West Virginia, most families lived in the midst of severe poverty. The birthrate was very high—2½ times the overall U.S. rate, and the same as India's birthrate. Living standards were low; the average family's purchasing power was about the same as a family in Malaysia. The typical house had just one or two rooms, and 60 percent of the reservation's dwellings had no electricity and 80 percent had no running water or sewers. Educational levels were low. The typical resident had completed just five years of school, and fewer than one adult in six had graduated high school. During World War II, Native Americans began to revolt against such conditions. In 1944, Native Americans formed the National Congress of American Indians (NCAI), the first major inter-tribal association. Among the group's primary concerns were protection of Indian land rights and improved educational opportunities for Native Americans. Congress voted in 1953 to allow states to assert legal jurisdiction over Indian reservations without tribal consent, and the federal government sought to transfer federal Indian responsibilities for a dozen tribes to the states (a policy known as "termination") and to relocate Indians into urban areas. The NCAI vehemently led opposition to these measures. "Self-determination rather than termination!" was the NCAI slogan. Earl Old Person, a Blackfoot leader, commented, "It is important to note that in our Indian language the only translation for termination is to 'wipe out' or 'kill off'.... How can we plan our future when the Indian Bureau threatens to wipe us out as a race? It's like trying to cook a meal in your tipi when someone is standing outside trying to burn the tipi down." By the late 1950s, a new spirit of Indian Nationalism had arisen. In 1959, the Tuscarora tribe, living in upstate New York, successfully resisted efforts by the state power authority to convert reservation land into a reservoir. In 1961, a militant new Indian organization, the National Indian Youth Council, appeared and began to use the phrase "Red Power." They sponsored demonstrations, marches, and "fish-ins" to protest state efforts to abolish Indian fishing rights guaranteed by federal treaties. In 1964, Native Americans in the San Francisco Bay area established the Indian Historical Society to present history from the Indian point of view. At the same time, the Native American Rights Fund brought legal suits against states that had taken Indian land and abolished Indian hunting, fishing, and water rights in violation of federal treaties. Many tribes also took legal action to prevent strip mining or spraying of pesticides on Indian lands. The best known of all Indian Power groups was the American Indian Movement (AIM), formed by a group of Chippewas in Minneapolis in 1966 to protest alleged police brutality. It began taking form in 1968 when 200 people from the Indian community turned out for a meeting called by a group of American Indian community activists led by George Mitchell, Dennis Banks, and Clyde Bellecourt. In the fall of 1972, AIM led urban Indians, traditionalists, and young Indians along the "Trail of Broken Treaties" to Washington, D.C., seized the offices of the Bureau of Indian Affairs, and occupied them for a week in order to dramatize Indian grievances. In the spring of 1973, a group of 200 heavily armed Indians took over the town of Wounded Knee, South Dakota—site of the 1890 massacre of 300 Sioux by the U.S. Army cavalry. The group of armed Indians occupied the town for 71 days. Militant protests paid off. The 1972 Indian Education Act gave Indian parents greater control over their children's schools. The 1976 Indian Health Care Act sought to address deficiencies in Indian health care, while the 1978 Indian Child Welfare Act gave tribes control over custody decisions involving Indian children. A series of landmark Supreme Court decisions aided the cause of Indian sovereignty and tribal self-government. The Williams v. Lee case (1959) upheld the authority of tribal courts to make decisions involving non-Indians. The Menominee Tribe v. United States case (1968) declared that states could not invalidate fishing and hunting rights that Indians had acquired through treaty agreements. Beginning in the 1970s, a number of tribes initiated lawsuits to recover land illegally seized by whites. In 1980, the federal government agreed to pay $81.5 million to the Passamaquoddy and Penobscot tribes of Maine, and $105 million to the Sioux in South Dakota. Court decisions also permitted tribal authorities to sell cigarettes, run gambling casinos, and levy taxes. The revolutionary fervor of AIM's leaders drew the attention of the FBI and the CIA, who then set out to crush the movement. Their ruthless suppression of AIM during the early 1970s sowed the seeds of the confrontation that followed in February, 1973, when AIM leader Russell Means and his followers took over the small Indian community of Wounded Knee (at the Pine Ridge reservation, SD), in protest of its allegedly corrupt government. When FBI agents were dispatched to remove the AIM occupiers, a standoff ensued. Through the resulting 71-day siege, two people were killed, twelve wounded, and twelve hundred arrested. Wounded Knee drew worldwide attention to the plight of American Indians. AIM leaders were later tried in a Minnesota court and, after a trial that lasted for eight months, were acquitted of wrongdoing. Richard Wilson's tribal leadership at the Pine Ridge reservation was reportedly federally sanctioned and supported. Allegations arose at the trials of AIM members that goon squad members were paid with BIA (Bureau of Indian Affairs) monies and that many of the members were in fact off-duty BIA police.

Several murders occurred on the reservation and were never fully investigated. For its part, the FBI maintained that it was an investigatory rather than an enforcement agency, a position that further exacerbated the regional tension and fear. In June 1975, two FBI agents in an unmarked car and clad in civilian clothes chased a pickup truck into an isolated area near an AIM encampment. During the resulting shootout, the two FBI agents were shot and killed, along with one Indian activist. Over the next several days, over 300 FBI agents swarmed the reservation, followed by officers making dozens of arrests and prosecutions.

AIM activist Leonard Peltier was tried and convicted for his role in the FBI killings, receiving two life sentences. His trial and conviction remained shrouded with allegations of suppressed evidence, coerced witnesses, and a fabricated murder weapon.[26]

ANNA MAE PICTOU AQUASH: On February 24, 1976, the frozen body of American Indian Movement (AIM) activist Anna Mae Pictou Aquash was found wrapped in a blanket. In a very unusual move, her hands were severed and sent to the FBI for fingerprinting and, even more unusual, she was quickly buried in a pauper's grave on March 3rd, before any identification was made. At her family's request, an exhumation order and a new autopsy was gained. On March 11, a second autopsy revealed the true cause of death—an execution shot to the back of the head and the .32 caliber bullet.

Theda Clark was the woman who first accused Aquash of being an informer at the 1975 AIM convention in New Mexico. At Looking Cloud's trial, FBI agent Price admitted that his job was to recruit informants, but that Anna Mae was not among them! John Trudell testified in Iowa June 22, 1976 that, "Dennis (Banks) told me she (Anna Mae) had been shot in the back of the head. He told me this in February, about the 25th or 26th of February." This was days before her body was found. Arlo Looking Cloud & John Boy Graham were both convicted of her murder in 2004 & 2010 and are now serving life. This has split AIM. Various AIM members have chosen sides as to who killed Aquash. Some AIM leaders have acknowledged that John Graham was the triggerman. To this day no one knows who killed her. Many believe it is a case of planting misleading information by the FBI that had her killed. Either way, Anna Mae Pictou Aquash was a genuine heroine. Her contributions to the cause of indigenous peoples are irrefutable.[27]

LATER YEARS: Following the Pine Ridge, Wounded Knee incident, AIM declined rapidly in both leadership and momentum. It held its last national unified event in 1978 and the following year dismantled as a national organization in favor of independent regional chapters. Russell Means and Dennis Banks were in and out of court for years, defending their leadership roles in the 1973 and 1975 shootouts. Eventually, both were acquitted of all significant charges. Dennis Banks went on to found another Indian organization, the Sacred Run, devoted to spiritual renewal and environmental issues. At the 1971 AIM national conference it was decided that translating policy into practice meant building organizations—schools and housing and employment services. Over the years, as the new organizations have grown, they have continued to serve the community from a base of Indian culture. Before AIM in 1968, culture had been weakened in most Indian communities due to U.S. policy, American boarding schools, and all the other efforts to extinguish Indian secular and spiritual life.

POSTSCRIPT—FACING THE FUTURE: In 2016 the American Indians are no longer a vanishing group of Americans. The 1990 census recorded an Indian population of over two Million—five times the number recorded in 1950. About half of these people live on reservations that cover 52.4 million acres in 27 states, while most others live in urban areas. The largest Native American populations are located in Alaska, Arizona, California, New Mexico, and Oklahoma. As the Indian population has grown in size, individual Indians have claimed many accomplishments; they are active leaders in theater, music, ballet, crafts, sports, etc.

Although American Indians continue to face severe problems related to employment, income and education, they have decisively demonstrated that they will not abandon their Indian identity and culture, nor will they be treated as dependent wards of the federal government. Indian communities still suffer from high rates of suicide, homicide, infant mortality, drug and alcohol abuse, poverty and the loss of culture, language, and spiritual practices. It has been a particular burden for the women and their children. Women have started to organize and form organizations to attempt to solve their many problems and protect their children from the drugs, gangs, rapes and epidemic of suicides.

Other activists are organizing to protect their indigenous rights, intellectual property, natural resources, border town hate crimes, and the unfairness of the justice system. The treaties that were forced upon them years ago are constantly being broken by the US and state governments in cahoots with large corporations and the Bureau of Indian Affairs (BIA). The BIA has always been a political organization acting not only from its own prejudices, but also at the behest of outsiders with power. These outsiders often wish to exploit the American Indians by taking their land and using the pretext of eminent domain, so as to mine their minerals as they pollute the Indians' water and air.

Boarding school survivors are in need of justice, peace, and reconciliation, and we need to continue to protect their sacred cites, repatriate the ceremonial objects and human remains, as well as protect the women and children from violence. The white man attempted to destroy their entire culture and language as well as break their spirit by taking their land and forcing them into reservations. Even worse were their efforts to change the Indian into a white man. In their attempt to do this, the white man has transferred all their diseases, drugs, alcohol and ways of life to the American Indian.

White European domination of the Americas has resulted in widespread environmental destruction. If there is any chance at all for the survival of humans and the rapidly disappearing flora and fauna of the planet, I am convinced that we must learn and apply all that we can from "the old ways." Why? Because the old ways worked. Although many have died by drugs, alcohol and suicides, the Indian spirit remains unbroken, as you can see from all the activists I have listed. There are many more appearing each day to fight for their freedom to become equal on their own terms in this white man's society. Unfortunately, at the present time, they are faced with another serious problem. It prevents their own people from putting through the changes they need. The white man has managed to bring greed and corruption to a number of their Chiefs and Council leaders, and have managed to turn the Have and Have-Nots against one another, as well as having this greed trickle down to the other residents of the reservation.

Isaac Rios, Pomo Indian/Illustrator/Poet, aptly explains this "divide and conquer" battle brought on by our present system, with many leaders catering to the establishment, in his poem:

PAPER CHIEFS

Fake native leaders misleading the people,
Putting communities down, treating them unequal,
Making crooked deals that are illegal;
Causing more drama then a soap opera sequel...
Saying they all had good intentions,
Seeing government money, their minds went in all kinds of directions,
Hiding federal audits from thorough inspections,
Using dis-enrollment as their only weapon.
It's hard for us grassroots people to be heard,
We be dealing with council members who don't live up to their word,
Labeled themselves traditional, which seems so absurd,
wearing eagle feathers they all didn't earn...
Pro-government who they choose to be,

Always the first ones to undermine our true beliefs,
Steady pulling scams for tax reliefs;
Now, to grassroots people, they're labeled as puppets & paper
chiefs!!!!

The families and the youth, especially in the reservation, are aware of all this and feel it is a hopeless situation for them as they are still dealing with the same old issues such as poverty, overcrowded homes, lack of educational opportunities, no access to healthy foods, no places to hang out and be kids, as well as few economic opportunities for their families, and suicides.

This new generation of youth has two choices: to surrender to all the bad temptations around them, or to stand up to fight for change, saying, "Enough is enough!" Many are joining forces with others of their tribe or getting in touch with many other youths all over the world (via the Internet) to seek a change.

As long as a majority of the people are looking for change, it is possible. America's Revolutionary War for independence, Irish independence, the fight to defeat South African apartheid, and the Civil Rights movement in the USA, etc., were all brought about by a determined few activists that began to challenge their oppressed system and living conditions. If we look back at all the resistance and successful changes, we find that they were brought about by a small core group of people seeking change. A survey (ready available) shows that approximately one percent of the population in these uprisings were active in their fight to change a corrupt system, as long as the majority supported them. Most of the remaining people were inactive supporters. Although small in size, when the core group managed to stay together it was possible to make a change. Staying resistant is not defeat—it has been the story of the American Indians for generations, continuously fighting to defend their past way of life for themselves and their children.

RACISM ON AND OFF AMERICAN INDIAN LANDS: Racism exists more than ever, on and off the reservation. Those Indians on reservations, particularly the young, face many obstacles due to extreme poverty, and low self-esteem. Outside of the reservations they are constantly watched, judged and blamed. The rash of suicides with the youth is one result of this racism.

A white man (or Wasichus – a Lakota name for non-Native people) who has witnessed it for over forty years, states:

"The kind of racism I have experienced on Indian lands by others of my own kind is just as, or more, insidious than any dictatorship. It is the banks and businessmen in SD [South Dakota] that perpetuate poverty and have allowed overt racism (Indians are stupid, backward, thieves, lazy, alcoholic, dirty, less than human beggars). This is what folks secretly believe that allows them to turn a blind eye to the criminal mistreatment (even baby thefts by the state for cash), which allows all of these injustices to go 'unnoticed.' There is not one Christian church in Rapid City that has any real relationship to people on the reservation. How? Why? Few ever question why hundreds of million of dollars are pumped into the Rapid City economy by American Indians day after day, year after year, and decade after decade (and into many other border towns), and yet they have never re-invested a dime, literally, and won't put a bank here because that would bring the federal re-investment act and upset the unchecked financial rape that goes on every day here. The grassroots Indians do not even have a local bank to place their savings, if any. The Indians have no choice but to shop in border town and the establishment keeps it that way so the Indian inhabitants never have the jobs that come with an internal economy. There are no Walmarts, shopping centers, etc. On the reservation it is a conspiracy that goes to the top of the power structure here. This is the reality of what goes on day after day in the Pine Ridge Indian reservation. We hear amazing racist and unconscious comments everyday from our liberal white friends! The poverty here, and I suspect in Wyoming and the Montana reservations, is absolutely purposeful! There is a cause—a powerfully motivated, ugly, economic purpose behind this horror—and it is financial! The U.S. government is only a small part of the problem. Regional greed and economics are behind the terrible quality of existence here and have been since the Pilgrim fathers died and their kids took over. If there was any reciprocity and South Dakota's re-invested in the folks who make the place rich, this would have been solved over a 100 years ago!! The most tragic result of the dispossessing of the American Indians into reservations has been the management and treating of Indians as if they are infants. All of this is managed by the Bureau of Indian Affairs (BIA) along with US government approval. Especially disastrous was to perpetuate this type of management where those on top receive the largest share, due to kickbacks given to those who supervise them. All this is known by those they are supposed to be serving. The result is apathy and discontent by those living on the reservations, along with more poverty; as well as not getting the services they were promised, such as taking care of the elderly, proper clinics, etc. Decolonized thinking for Indian people actually results in a much longer historical perspective, like waiting for the current regime called the United States of America to collapse of its own pollution, racism, anger, internal violence, and daily corruption—self-murder by guns, criminal behavior, spiritual bankruptcy and extreme greed. What comes next when the skin color of America is brown, besides a new flag? They will start to dig up old colonial era Wasp grave yards, examine the remains the buttons and bones, and then put the bones in a new "American Museum of the Ancient Order." Folks will go to the museum to learn about an imperialistic society that used wage slavery to prop itself up until that God-awful, apocalyptic day when Walmart could no longer sell Chinese made facsimiles of products that the poor could afford (like a limited warrantee on a realistic, high-definition poster of a window fan: "Just paste it over your window and you will believe you are cooler!"), McDonald's runs out of realistic-looking processed burgers, the beach moves inland 20 miles, and the class and race riots begin. When, years later, the noise settles down, our descendants will go out exploring and take a look at the mortifying remains of that terrible failed experiment and the folks who brought all that mess here. Maybe they will cry... or more likely, they will give just give a tiny, wry chuckle. Presently, what the white man hates most is that Indians are the real true Americans and do not want to be white. "They are going to hang another Indian before the white man takes the blame," holds true—especially out West, where a scapegoat is needed. Their crime in the eyes of the whites is that they are still here and inhabit land given to them in treaties that many whites would love go and take for themselves. The same similar story takes place every day in America with any minority; Asians, Blacks, Hispanics, Jews, Muslims, and indigenous peoples throughout the world. Racism is a learned behavior. The very young don't see different colors. There are good and bad people in all cultures and races. They all are facing these same prejudices. Living with it in America destroys the very fabric of Liberty and Equality that this nation was built on. What our world needs right now is to have, and treasure, all these minorities and indigenous cultures, without continuously murdering it with greed, bigotry and hate."

AMERICAN INDIAN ACTIVISM

Time-Line of Important Events

1950s – Wallace "Mad Bear" Anderson was a Tuscarora leader in New York. He struggled to resist the New York City planner Robert Moses' plan to take tribal land in upstate New York for use in a state hydropower project to supply New York City. The struggle ended in a bitter compromise.

1954 – Fish-Ins: First arrest occurred in 1954. Robert Satiacum was arrested for gill netting without a license and out of season. The case continued up to Washington's Supreme Court. It was eventually dropped, but had a lasting effect. The decision by lower courts suggested that the State had the jurisdiction to regulate Indian fishing.

1964, February – Fish-Ins: Tribal leaders met with members of the NCAI and the NIYC. They decided to take action to protect treaty rights. *How* to protest became a topic of contention, because many feared their cause would become linked with the American Indian civil rights movement, which was occurring at the same time. March 3, 1964, a NIYC-planned protest occurred in Olympia, Washington. Somewhere between 1,500 to 5,000 people attended, making it the largest inter-tribal protest to date. Clyde Warrior declared that fish-in protesting was establishing "the beginning of a new era in the history of American Indians."

In the end, the fish-ins of March 1964 did not bring about immediate change, but they attracted members of more than 45 tribes, helping build a pan-Native American movement. Many of NIYC's members called them the "greatest Indian victory of the modern day." Finally, in 1974, the United States Supreme Court closed *United States v. Washington* to further review. The decision mandated that the treaty Indians had gave them the right to catch 50% of Washington's harvested fish.

1968 – March 6: In a special message to Congress, President Lyndon Baines Johnson announced that, "the time has come to focus our efforts on the plight of the American Indian." He told Congress that the United States was now in a position "to deal with the persistent problems of the American Indian" since the enactment of "recent landmark laws" such as the Elementary and Secondary Education Act, Economic Opportunity Act, and the Manpower Development and Training Act. He added a moral component: "No enlightened nation, no responsible government, no progressive people, can sit idly by and permit this shocking situation to continue." In conjunction with this speech to the U.S. Congress, President Johnson signed Executive Order 11399 establishing the National Council on Indian Opportunity (NCIO). He pledged that the NCIO's formation would "launch an undivided, government-wide effort" in order to allow American Indians to gain "full participation in the life of modern America."

1969 – November, Alcatraz Island: After previous attempts by activists of all tribes, 79 Indians, including students, married couples and six children, returned to Alcatraz to claim their right to the island under the Fort Laramie Treaty of 1868.

1970 – Legal rights Center: Created to assist in alleviating legal issues facing Indian people. (In 1994, over 19,000 clients have had legal representation, thanks to AIM's founding of the Legal Rights Center.)

1972 – Red School House: The second survival school to open, offering culturally-based education services to K-12 students in St. Paul, MN.

1972 – November: AIM brought a caravan of Native Nation representatives to the Department of Interior, Washington, DC, to declare the following claims of theirs, directly to the President of the United States:

Restoration of treaty making (ended by Congress in 1871).

Establishment of a treaty commission to make new treaties (with sovereign Native Nations). Indian leaders to address Congress.

Review of treaty commitments and violations.

Treaties not ratified to go before the Senate.

All Indians to be governed by treaty relations.

Relief for Native Nations for treaty rights violations.

Recognition of the right of Indians to interpret treaties.

Joint Congressional Committee to be formed on reconstruction of Indian relations.

Restoration of 110 million acres of land taken away from Native Nations by the United States.

Restoration of terminated rights.

Repeal of state jurisdiction on Native Nations.

Resume Federal protective jurisdiction for offenses against Indians.

Abolishment of the Bureau of Indian Affairs.

Creation of a new office of Federal Indian Relations.

New office to remedy the breakdown in the constitutionally prescribed relationships between the United States and Indian Nations. Indian Nations need to be immune to commerce regulation, taxes, and trade restrictions of states. Indian religious freedom and cultural integrity has to be protected.

Establishment of national Indian voting with local options; free national Indian organizations from governmental controls.

Reclaim and affirm health, housing, employment, economic development, and education for all Indian people.

1973 – Wounded Knee: AIM was contacted by Lakota elders for assistance in dealing with the corruption within the BIA and Tribal Council, which led to the famed 71-day occupation and battle with U.S. armed forces.

1973 – Feb. 27, Wounded Knee Trials: Eight months of trials in Minneapolis resulted from events which occurred during the Wounded Knee occupation. This was the longest Federal trial in the history of the United States. Many instances of government misconduct were revealed, with the result being that US District Judge Fred Nichol dismissed all charges due to government "misconduct," which "formed a pattern throughout the course of the trial" so that "the waters of justice have been polluted."

1973 – Little Earth of United Tribes: Little Earth is the only American Indian preference project, based on Section 8 rental assistance. HUD chose AIM to be the prime sponsor of the first Indian-run housing project.

1973 – Trial of Banks and Means: Russell Means and Dennis Banks were arrested, but on September 16, 1973, the charges against them were dismissed by a federal judge due to the U.S. government's unlawful handling of witnesses and evidence. After an eight-and-a-half-month trial, the U.S. District Court of South Dakota (Fred Joseph Nichol, presiding judge) dismissed the charges against Banks and Means for conspiracy and assault (both Banks and Means were defended by William Kunstler and Mark Lane).

1974 – International Indian Treaty Council (IITC): An organization representing Indian peoples throughout the western hemisphere at the United Nations in Geneva, Switzerland.

1975-1977 – Two FBI agents and a Native man were killed in a shoot-out between federal agents, AIM members and local residents. In 1976 Leonard Peltier was arrested. The trial was held in 1977 in North Dakota before United States District Judge Paul Benson, a conservative judge appointed to the federal bench by Richard M. Nixon. In the trial that followed, the jury unanimously concluded, on April 18, 1977, that AIM member Leonard Peltier was guilty of two counts of murder in the first degree and sentenced to two consecutive life terms.

1978 – First education programs for American Indian offenders: AIM establishes the first adult education program at Stillwater prison in Minnesota. Programs were later established at other state correctional facilities modeled after the Minnesota program.

1978 – Run for Survival: AIM Youth organize and conduct a 500-mile run from Minneapolis to Lawrence, Kansas to support "the longest walk."

1978 – The Longest Walk: Indian nations walk across the U.S. from California to Washington, DC to protest Anti-Indian legislation calling for the abrogation of treaties. A tipi is set up and maintained on the grounds of the White House. The proposed Anti-Indian legislation is defeated.

1978 – Women of All Red Nations (WARN): Established to address issues directly facing Indian women and their families.

1978 – Congress passes the American Indian Religious Freedom Act (AIRFA) (42 U.S. C.A 1996): Designed to review and update federal policies regarding such matters as Native Americans' right to access sacred grounds and legal rights to practice their traditional religions. Reviews and recommendations were made. Pursuant to this action, Congress in 1990 passed the Native American graves protection and repatriation act, but in that same year, the U.S. Supreme Court reiterated its 1988 ruling that AIRFA was a policy statement and not law and, as such, there was no legal right to the protection of sacred sites or the religious use of peyote in the Native American religion.

1979 – Little Earth Housing Protected: An attempt by the US Department of Housing and Urban Development to foreclose on the Little Earth of United Tribes housing project is halted by legal action and the US District Court issues an injunction against HUD.

1979 – American Indian Opportunities Industrialization Center (AIOIC): Creates job training schools to attack the outrageous unemployment issues of Indian people. Over 17,000 Native Americans have been trained for jobs since AIM created the American Indian Opportunities Industrialization Center.

1979 – Anishinabe Akeeng Organization is created to regain stolen and tax-forfeited land on the White Earth Reservation in Minnesota.

1986 – Schools Lawsuit: Heart of the Earth and Red School House successfully sue the U.S. Department of Education, Indian Education Programs for unfairly ranking the schools' programs below funding recommendation levels. The schools proved bias in the system of ranking by the Department staff.

1987 – AIM Patrol: Minneapolis AIM Patrol comes full circle in restarting the Patrol to deal with the serial killings of American Indian women in Minneapolis.

1988 – Elaine Stately Indian Youth Services (ESIYS): Developed to create alternatives for youth as a direct diversion to gang involvement of Indian youth.

1989 – Spearfishing: AIM is requested to provide expertise in dealing with angry protesters on boat landings. Spearfishing continues despite violence, arrests, and threats from white racists. Senator Daniel Inouye calls for a study on the effects of Indian spearfishing. The study shows only 6% of fish taken are by Indians. Sports fishing accounts for the rest.

1990 – Native American Languages Act: The short cited title for executive order Public Law-101-477, enacted by Congress on October 30, 1990. This law was of historical importance as it repudiated past policies of eradicating Indian languages by declaring, as policy, that Native Americans were entitled to use their own languages. In addition, it allowed to "fully recognize the right of Indian Tribes and other Native American governing bodies, States, territories, and possessions of the United States to take action on, and give official status to their Native American languages for the purpose of conducting their own business."

1991 – Peacemaker Center: Created as an American Indian spiritual base. AIM houses its AIM Patrol and ESIYS in a center in the heart of the Indian community.

1991 – Separate Nation: Leaders of the Oglala Lakota, Cheyenne and other nations declared independence from the United States. The group established a provisional government and began the other work of developing a separate nation.

1992 – National Coalition on Racism in Sports and Media: Organized to address the use of Indians as sports team mascots.

1992 – The Food Connection: Summer youth jobs program is organized with an organic garden and spiritual camp (Common Ground) at Tonkawood Farm in Orono, MN.

1993 – Expansion of American Indian OIC Job Training Program: The Grand Metropolitan, Inc. of Great Britain, a parent of the Pillsbury Corporation, merges its job-training program with that of AIOIC and pledges future monies and support.

1994 – Minneapolis Star-Tribune agrees to stop using professional sports team names that refer to Indian people.

1996 – April 3-8, Preparatory Meeting for the Intercontinental Encounter for Humanity: As a representative of the American Indian Movement Grand Governing Council (AIMGGC) and special representative of the International Indian Treaty Council, Vernon Bellecourt, along with William A. Means, President of IITC, attended.

1998 – February 27, Liberation Day: Established on 25th Anniversary of the Wounded Knee uprising. This was an Oglala Lakota Nation resolution, established February 27th, as a National Day of Liberation.

1998 – July 16-19, 25th Annual Lac Courte Oreilles Honor the Earth Homecoming Celebration: Created to celebrate and honor the people of the American Indian Movement and those of Lac Courte Oreilles who participated in the July 31, 1971 takeover of the Winter Dam and the birth of Honor the Earth.

1998 – August 2-11, 30th Anniversary of the American Indian Movement, Grand Governing Council; Sacred Pipestone Quarries in Pipestone, Minnesota: Welcoming Feast and Celebration/Conference commemorating AIM's 30th Anniversary.

2000 – October: Commission to seek justice for Ingrid Washinawatok and companions established.

2001 – March: Representatives of the American Indian Movement Grand Governing Council attend the **Zapatista Army of National Liberation March for Peace, Justice and Dignity**, Zocolo Plaza, Mexico City.

2001 – July: 11th Annual Youth & Elders International Cultural Gathering and Sundance; Pipestone, Minnesota.

2001 – August: Civil lawsuit for false arrest brought by five anti-wahoo demonstrators against the city of Cleveland.

2001 – November: The American Indian Forum on Racism in Sports and Media, Black Bear Crossing, St. Paul, Minnesota.

2002 – August: 12th Annual International Youth & Elders Cultural Gathering and Sundance, Pipestone, Minnesota.

2003 – May: Quarterly Meeting of the AIM National Board of Directors, Thunderbird House, Winnipeg, Manitoba.

2003 – August: 13th Annual International Youth & Elders Cultural Gathering and Sundance, Pipestone, Minnesota.

2003 – Russell Means, campaigning for governor of New Mexico as an independent, was barred from the ballot.

2004 – August: 14th Annual International Youth & Elders Cultural Gathering and Sundance, Honor Your Grandparents; Wisdom Keeper of Tomorrow; Pipestone, Minnesota.

2005 – May: First Annual Clyde H. Bellecourt Endowment Scholarship Fund and Awards Banquet, Minneapolis Convention Center.

2005 – July: 15th Annual International Youth & Elders Cultural Gathering and Sundance, International Prayer Vigil for the Earth, Pipestone, Minnesota.

2006 – Dennis Banks led **Sacred Run 2006**, a spiritual run from San Francisco's Alcatraz Island to Washington, D.C.

2006 – July: 16th Annual International Youth & Elders Cultural Gathering and Sundance; Pipestone, Minnesota.

2007 – Means and 80 other protesters were arrested in Denver during a parade for Columbus Day, which they stated was a "celebration of genocide."

2007 – June: Information from a whistleblower was given to GAO's Fraud NET hotline alleging millions of dollars in lost and stolen property and gross mismanagement of property at Indian Health Service (IHS), an operating division of the Department of Health and Human Services Millions of dollars worth of IHS property had been lost or stolen over the previous several years. Specifically, IHS identified over 5,000 lost or stolen property items worth about $15.8 million from fiscal years 2004 through 2007. It was not until 2016 before the government begins talks on making changes.

2007 – September 13: The United Nations adopts the **Declaration on the Rights of Indigenous Peoples,** which has since been ratified by 143 countries. Later, on December 20, a group of American Indian activists presented a letter to the U.S. State Department, indicating they were withdrawing from all treaties with the U.S. government. Russell Means and a delegation of activists declared the Republic of Lakotah a sovereign nation, with property rights over thousands of square miles in S. Dakota, N. Dakota, Nebraska, Wyoming & Montana.

2011 – August: The Keystone XL Pipeline Protesters Launch Massive Campaign. Environmental and indigenous groups launched a massive campaign designed to press President Obama not to approve the Keystone XL Pipeline project that would run through and near tribal lands, water resources, and places of spiritual significance. After massive protests on Nov. 6, 2015, President Obama rejected the Keystone XL Pipeline proposal.

2012 – Dec. 30, Pine Ridge, South Dakota: Vowing, "We will live up to our obligation once again and be idle no more," **Oglala Lakota Women** and allies from the **Deep Green Resistance** blockaded the border of Pine Ridge and White Clay, Nebraska, to prevent alcohol from entering the Pine Ridge Reservation where sales, possession and consumption are illegal.

2013 – March 7: The Havasupai Tribe, along with three conservation groups, filed a lawsuit against the U.S. Forest Service "over its decision to allow Energy Fuels Resources, Inc. to begin operating a uranium mine near Grand Canyon National Park without initiating or completing formal tribal consultations and without updating an outdated 1986 federal environmental review." In April 2015, a U.S. District Judge ruled on this suit and decided uranium mining can continue in Northern Arizona.

2014 – August 13: State Sen. Randy Baumgardner, Colorado state legislator, has dismissed concerns about hydraulic fracturing polluting water with methane as "propaganda," saying that it's natural to have methane in water. He said that methane actually helped Native Americans.

2014 – December 9, House Votes To Sell Apache Land To Foreign Corporation: For over 5 years, a measure to cede 2,400 acres sacred to the Apache tribe for use in copper mining has been pushed through in Congress. The land in question is part of the Tonto National Forest in Arizona. The legislation was backed by various well-paid, pro-corporate Congress members such as Senator John McCain.

2015 – June 26, 40th Anniversary of the 1975 *Incident at Oglala* (portrayed in a 1992 documentary by Michael Apted, narrated by Robert Redford). The killings of the two FBI agents are what led up to this incident on the Pine Ridge Reservation in South Dakota, during what has become known as the "Reign of Terror" among the Lakota and other American Indian tribes. Greed by both local tribal members and the United States Federal Government, which included the United States Bureau of Indian Affairs (BIA) and the United States Federal Bureau of Investigation (FBI), were responsible for this act of domestic terrorism, as they attempted to open the Pine Ridge reservation to mining exploration.

2015 – August 5: The EPA reported that crews at a defunct gold mine in southern Colorado, the Gold King Mine near Silverton, accidentally released more than three million gallons of highly contaminated water into Cement Creek, a tributary of the Animas River. The "River of Souls" is a critical source of agricultural water and its' rights for Native farmers from the Ute and Navajo (Diné) nations.

2015 – October 20: Canada's Liberal Party leader, Justin Trudeau, promises to establish a new "nation to nation" relationship with indigenous peoples.

2015 – Wounded Knee: December 29th marks the 125th anniversary of when 300 or more innocent and unarmed Lakota men, women, children, infants, and elders were gunned down by the United States 7th Cavalry at Wounded Knee Creek in South Dakota. Nearly a century following the massacre, history books finally acknowledged that what occurred at Wounded Knee was not a battle, but an all-out massacre.

2016 – January 26: An audit of 23 of the Navajo Nation's 110 chapters has found that mismanagement cost the tribe $10.8 million in lost revenue related to internal controls and compliance with Navajo, state and federal laws.

2016 – Feb. 6, Associated Press: A judge in New Mexico has approved a nearly $1 billion settlement between the Obama administration and American Indian tribes over claims that the government shorted tribes on contracts to manage education, law enforcement and other federal services.

2016 – March 4, Climate Change: February was the warmest month on record. The number of people who could be displaced in U.S. coastal regions due to rising sea levels this century, as a result of climate change, is much higher than previously thought. More than 13 million Americans are at risk of a 6-foot (1.8 meters) rise, including 6 million people in Florida. Scientists have estimated that by 2050, 500,000 people worldwide will die due to decimating crops.

2016 – March 13: Mohawks threaten to block Energy East. The Grand Chief of the Kanesatake Mohawks, Serge Simon, says the Energy East pipeline project "is a threat to our way of life. We reserve the right to take legal action if necessary to prevent the abuse of our inherent rights."

2016 – March 10: The Bureau of Indian Affairs placed a sacred site in the Black Hills of South Dakota in trust. The Crow Creek Sioux Tribe, the Rosebud Sioux Tribe, the Shakopee Mdewakanton Sioux Community, and the Standing Rock Sioux Tribe raised $9 million to purchase Pe' Sla, a 2,022-acre site that plays a central role in Lakota history, culture and cosmology.

2016 – March 21: A woman asks for help with water pollution from a Cree Indian community in Canada. "We need help in our community; there is bad water, the kids are getting rashes. We are here in

Canada, Ontario. Our reservation is called Kashechewan, located in James Bay Area."

2016 – March 24, Iowa Tribes of Kansas and Nebraska are objecting to the **Dakota Access Pipeline:** The 1,100-mile pipeline by Energy Transfer Partners would start in the Bakken oil fields in North Dakota and would cross South Dakota before entering Iowa and ending in Illinois. The route crosses aboriginal and treaty-ceded lands that traverse the entire state. Tribes in North Dakota and South Dakota are also fighting the project, comparing it to the Keystone XL Pipeline that President Barack Obama killed in November of 2015.

2016 – April 3, Panama Papers: A huge leak of confidential documents has revealed the rich and powerful use tax havens to hide their wealth. The documents show links to 72 current or former heads of state accused of looting their own countries.

2016 – Leonard Peltier remains in prison. The FBI still refused to release nearly 6,000 pages of documents on Peltier, being withheld on grounds of "national security." [28]

2016 – Apr 27, Pine Ridge, S.D. Under intense pressure to improve its performance, the Indian Health Service will now turn to outside managers to run its emergency room at its Pine Ridge and other hospitals, tribal leaders say.

PHOTOS OF AMERICAN INDIANS PAST AND PRESENT

Navajo
1917-2012
Harrison Begay
Painter

Edmonia Lewis -Ojibwe
Sculptor
1844-1907

John Herrington
Chickasaw
Astronaut

Chief Gall-Lakota
1840-1894

AMERICAN INDIAN CHIEFS

Geronimo Apache 1829-1909

Chief Little Coyote

Chief Dull Knife (Morning Star) 1810-1883 Cheyenne

Chief Big Foot - Wife Lakota White Hawk 1825-1890

Red Cloud 1822-1909 Lakota

Chief Wooden Leg 1858-1940 Cheyenne

Chief Captain Jack Modoc 1837-1873

Chief Ouray -Ute 1833-1880

Chief Little Crow 1810-1863

119

AMERICAN INDIAN ATHLETES

Lewis Tewanima
Hopi Tribe (1888-1969), New York City marathon win, 1911

Jim Thorpe
1888-1953
Sac & Fox

Billy Mills
Lakota
1938-

AMERICAN INDIAN BALLET, SINGER & ACTOR

Maria Tallchief 1925-2013
Osage

Yvonne Chouteau
1929-2016
Shawnee-Cherokee

Rita Coolidge
Cherokee
Songwriter
Singer

Marcos Akiaten
APACHE
1948-2010

AMERICAN INDIAN WAR HEROS

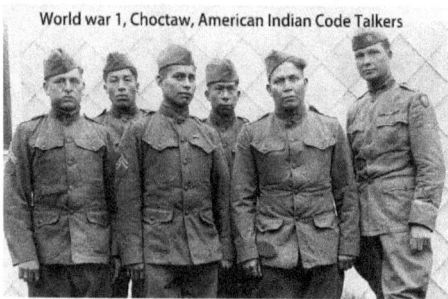

Ira Hayes -Pima
Marine War Hero
Flag Raising- Iwo Jima
1923-1955

Medal of Honor

World War 11
Korea
Sisseton Wahpeton Oyate
(Lakota)

Woodrow W. Keeble
1917-1982

Chief Medicine Crow
1913-2016
WAR HERO

Presidential Medal
of Honor

World war 1, Choctaw, American Indian Code Talkers

AMERICAN INDIAN ACTORS, ARTISTS, POETS

Actor
Poet

Chief Dan George
Geswanouth Slahoot
Tsleil-Waututh First Nation, 1899-1981

Wilt Sampson
Muscogee

Buffy St. Marie
Cree First Nation

Zitkala-Sa
1876-1938

Lakota
writer, editor
musician, teacher
& .political activist

Will Rogers
Cherokee
1879-1935

AMERICAN INDIAN ARTIST; AUTHORS

Sarah Winnemucca 1844-1891
Paiute
Author

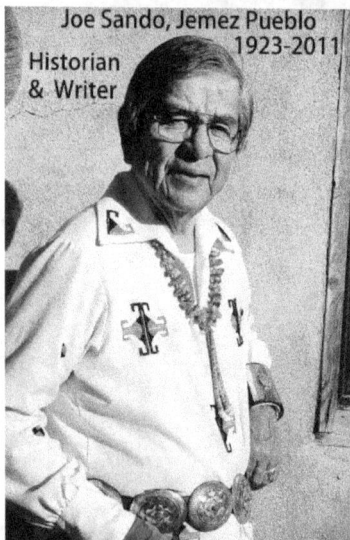

Paula Gunn Allen
Laguna Pueblo 1939-2008

Joe Sando, Jemez Pueblo 1923-2011
Historian
& Writer

Darren Vigil Gray
Apache
1959-   Artist

INDIAN ACTIVISTS AND CHIEF

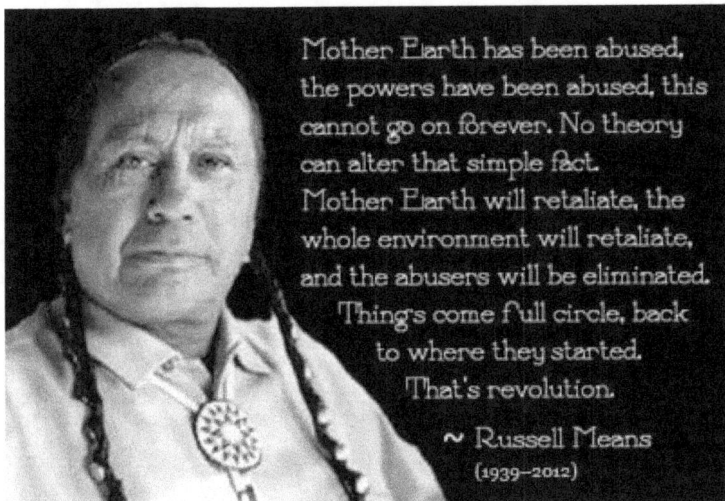

Mother Earth has been abused, the powers have been abused, this cannot go on forever. No theory can alter that simple fact. Mother Earth will retaliate, the whole environment will retaliate, and the abusers will be eliminated. Things come full circle, back to where they started. That's revolution.

~ Russell Means
(1939–2012)

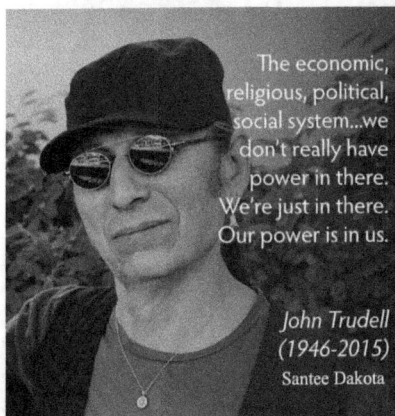

The economic, religious, political, social system...we don't really have power in there. We're just in there. Our power is in us.

John Trudell
(1946-2015)
Santee Dakota

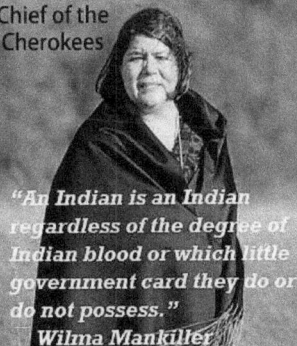

1945-2010
Chief of the Cherokees

"An Indian is an Indian regardless of the degree of Indian blood or which little government card they do or do not possess."
Wilma Mankiller

INDIAN ACTIVISTS, SINGER, ACTOR & WRITER

HONOR THE EARTH

Love Water not Oil. Time to evolve past fossil fuels.
— Winona LaDuke

Buffy Sainte-Marie -Cree
Singer - Activist

Floyd "Red Crow" Westerman
Lakota
1936-2007
musician
actor
activist

Mary Brave Bird
1954-2013
lakota
Writer
Activist

ACTOR & DIRECTOR- PHYSICIAN/ AUTHOR

WES STUDI
Cherokee
Actor

Chris Eyre
Cheyenne-Arapaho
Director

Charles Eastman

Author   Physician
Santee Dakota
1858- 1939

NAMES OF HEROIC AMERICAN INDIAN ACTIVISTS

(With Many More Unsung Heroes Too Numerous To Mention)

Hank Adams, Paula Gunn Allen, Wallace "Mad Bear" Anderson, Apesanahkwat, Anna Mae Aquash, Mary Ellicott Arnold, Dennis Banks, Clyde Bellecourt, Klee Benally, Selo Black Crow, Amanda Blackhorse, Cindy Blackstock, Eunice Bommelyn, John Boncore, Mary Brave Bird, Carter Camp, Ed Castillo, Hiram Chase, Wendell Chino, Choctaw Youth Movement, Radmilla Cody, Lyda Conley, Elizabeth Cook-Lynn, Sherman Coolidge, Sarah Adams-Cornell, Chester Poe Cornelius, Rod Coronado, Lucy Covington, Leonard Crow Dog, Charles Edwin Dagenett, Mary Dann, Carrie Dann, Lorelei DeCora Means, Joe DeLaCruz, Vine Deloria, Jr., Deskaheh, John EchoHawk, Charlotte Black Elk, Dan Evehema, Pura Fé, Cecilia Fire Thunder, Adam Fortunate Eagle, Billy Frank, Jr., Kalyn Free, Tom B.K. Goldtooth, Philip B. Gordon, Roxy Gordon, Saginaw Grant, Thomas Greenwood (activist), Francella Mary Griggs, Tillie Hardwick, Suzan Shown Harjo, Corbin Harney, LaDonna Harris, Harry Hill (activist), Cheryll Toney Holley, Kahn-Tineta Horn, Zilphia Horton, Dresden Howard, Ralph Hubbard, Chase Iron Eyes, Alice Lee Jemison, Thomasina Jordan, Dan Katchongva, Laura Cornelius Kellogg, Susette La Flesche, Winona LaDuke, Carole LaFavor, Agnes White Buffalo Chief LaMonte, John Fire Lame Deer, Ernie Lapointe, Roberta Lawson, Ronald G. Lewis, Sacheen Littlefeather, Chief Arvol Looking Horse, Jacqueline Keeler (TiyospayeNow), Beatrice Long Visitor Holy Dance (Council of the International Council of 13 Indigenous Grandmothers), Rita Long Visitor Holy Dance, Henry Berry Lowrie, Ronnie Lupe, Oren Lyons, Wilma Mankiller, Tina Manning, Olowan

S.Martinez, Janet McCloud, Ashley Nicole McCray, D'Arcy McNickle, Russell Means, Devon A. Mihesuah, Minnie Two Shoes, Sara Misquez, David Monongye, Nas'Naga, Darlene Ka-Mook, Nichols Mildred Noble, Richard Oakes, Lucy Parsons, Maria Pearson, Leonard Peltier, Aurelius H. Piper, Sr., Pun Plamondon, Simon Pokagon, Luana Reyes, G. Anne Richardson, Clinton Rickard, Frankie Rivera, Robert Roche, Luana Ross, Yvette Roubideaux, Clarence Rowland, Katherine Siva Saubel, Thomas L. Sloan, Redbird Smith, Donald Soctomah, Loren Spears, Henry Standing Bear, Luther Standing Bear, Nipo T. Strongheart, Ralph W. Sturges, Sundance (activist), Jo Ann Tall, Eloisa Garcia Tamez, Margo Tamez, Billy Redwing Tayac, Charlene Teters, Mel Thom, Mary Thomas (politician), Grace Thorpe, Madonna Thunder Hawk, Thomas Tibbles, Dana Tiger, Catherine Troeh, John Trudell, Asiba Tupahache, Richard Two Elk, Billy Ray Waldon, Clyde Warrior Della Warrior, Ingrid Washinawatok, Annie Dodge Wauneka, Waziyatawin, Summer Wesley, Floyd Red Crow Westerman, Mahomet Weyonomon, Dennison Wheelock, Charmaine White Face, Albert White Hat, Bernie Whitebear, Sarah Winnemucca, Chauncey Yellow Robe, Philip Yenyo, Phylis Young, Zitkala-Sa.

AMERICAN INDIAN RIGHTS ORGANIZATIONS

Alaskan Native Brotherhood and Sisterhood
Alaska Federation of Natives
American Indian College Fund
American Indian Defense Association
American Indian Federation
American Indian Movement
Choctaw Youth Movement
Four Mothers Society
Indigenous Life Movement
Indian Rights Association
Inter-Tribal Environmental Council
Keetoowah Nighthawk Society
Not Your Mascots.org.
Mohawk Warrior Society
Mothers Against METH Alliance
National American Indian Council
Native American Youth Standing Strong (NAYSS)
National Congress of American Indians
National Council of American Indians
National Indian Education Association
National Indian Youth Council
Native American Rights Fund
Society of American Indians
White Earth Land Recovery Project

FILMS FAVORABLE TO AMERICAN INDIANS

Daughter of Dawn: 1920. Silent film that tended to romanticize American Indian culture and lifestyle during the early 1910s and '20s. It was filmed in Oklahoma and featured an all-Indian cast, with over 300 people from the Comanche and Kiowa tribes acting in the film, including White and Wanada Parker, children of Quannah Parker. The cast wore their own clothing and brought their own personal items, including teepees.

Soldier Blue: 1970. Inspired by the 1864 Sand Creek massacre in the Colorado Territory. Film is a graphic version of the rape and savage slaughter of American Indians by American soldiers.

Powwow Highway: 1989. Activist is battling greedy developers. Takes place on the Northern Cheyenne Indian Reservation.

Dead Man: 1995. Johnny Depp, before he took on his caricature Native American role in Disney's 2013 *The Lone Ranger*. Directed by Jim Jarmusch, this black-and-white movie is rather anti-Western and deconstructs the traditional Western cliches that came before it.

Smoke Signals: 1998. Cheyenne-Arapaho film director Chris Eyre directed. This revolutionary movie "paved the way for other American Indian artists to reach similar success as they combat the traditional Native American stereotypes created by the popular media," according to Cultural Survival. *Smoke Signals* is based on Spokane-Coeur d'Alene writer Sherman Alexie's short story collection, *The Lone Ranger and Tonto Fistfight in Heaven.*

Atanarjuat: The Fast Runner: 2001. A Canadian epic film directed by Inuit filmmaker Zacharias Kunuk and produced by his production company, Isuma Igloolik Productions. It was the first feature film ever to be written, directed and acted entirely in Inuktitut. Set in the ancient past, it tells an Inuit legend of an evil spirit causing strife in the community and one warrior's endurance and battle of its menace.

Bury My Heart at Wounded Knee: 2007. Television film adapted from the book of the same name by Dee Brown. The book on which the movie is based is a history of Native Americans in the West in the 1860s and 1870s, focusing upon the transition from traditional ways of living to living on reservations and their treatment during that period.

Reel Injun: 2009. Traces the evolution of cinema's depiction of American Indian people from the silent film era to today. A sobering yet humorous documentary by Cree filmmaker Neil Diamond, looking at the history of Hollywood's portrayal of American Indians—from glorification to the downright violent and ridiculous.

Barking Water: 2009. Film by Sterlin Harjo, a Seminole/Creek director and writer (who also directed the Netflix-streamable documentary, *This May Be the Last Time*, 2014). *Barking Water* is about the privilege of redemption.

On the Ice: 2011. Drama-thriller directed by Alaskan Andrew Okpeaha MacLean. *On the Ice* is a coming-of-age story set in Alaska, which focuses on the friendship of two Inuit boys from vastly different backgrounds, who must live through the consequences of an accident and the choices that follow.

Winter in the Blood: 2013. An adaptation from a 1974 novel by Great Plains Indian writer, James Welch. The directors, twin brothers Alex and Andrew Smith, grew up in rural Montana and are close family friends with Welch. They signed up Spokane-Coeur d'Alene writer, Sherman Alexie, as the associate producer. An unflinching look at the problems of alcoholism on the reservation.

Urban Rez: 2013. Explores the controversial legacy and modern-day repercussions of the Urban Relocation Program (1952-1973), the greatest voluntary upheaval of American Indians during the 20th century.

Buffalo Nation: The Children Are Crying: 2014. Written by Leslye Abbey, this is a documentary film that depicts the tragic way of life for the rural, isolated Lakota people living on the Pine Ridge Indian Reservation in South Dakota. This documentary focuses on the devastation in which the children of the Lakota Sioux Nation are forced to live. The children are filled with despair and, as a result, they are committing suicide at an alarming rate. They are crying for help!

Crying Earth Rise Up: 2015. A documentary film project exploring contaminated water and the impact of uranium mining on the people of the Great Plains.

BOOKS FAVORABLE TO AMERICAN INDIANS

Seth K. Humphrey, *The Indian Dispossessed,* Boston, Little Brown & Co., 1905.

Helen Jackson, *A Century of Dishonor,* Indian Head Books, NY. N.Y. 1994.

M. Annette James, Editor, *The State of Native America, Genocide, Colonization and Resistance,* South End Press, Boston, Ma.1992.

Dee Brown, *Bury My Heart at Wounded Knee:* New York: Holt, Rinehart, & Winston.

The New Warriors: Native American Leaders Since 1900, Lincoln: University of Nebraska Press, 2001.

Alvin M. Josephy, Jr., *The Patriot Chiefs: A Chronicle of American Indian Resistance,* Lincoln: University of Nebraska Press, 1984.

Alvin M. Josephy, Jr., two-volume set, *The Great Father: The United States Government and the American Indians,* Berkeley: University of California Press, 1985.

Anthony F. C. Wallace, *Jefferson and the Indians: The Tragic Fate of the First Americans,* Cambridge, Massachusetts: The Belknap Press of Harvard University Press, 1999. Concludes that Jeffersonian Indian policy produced "ethnic cleansing."

Frederick E. Hoxie, *A Final Promise: The Campaign to Assimilate the Indians,* 1880-1920, Lincoln: University of Nebraska Press, 1984.

Donald Lee Fixico, *Termination and Relocation: Federal Indian Policy, 1945-1960,* Albuquerque: University of New Mexico Press, 1986.

Wilcomb E. Washburn, *Red Man's Land, White Man's Law,* Charles Scribner & Sons, New York, 1971.

Debo, *And Still the Waters Run,* Princeton University Press.

Utley, *The Last Days of the Sioux Nation,* New Haven: Yale University Press, 1963.

John G. Neihardt, *Black Elk Speaks: Being the Life Story of a Holy Man of the Oglala Sioux,* New York: William Morrow and Company, 1932.

Vin Deloria, *Custer Died for Your Sins: An Indian Manifesto,* New York: Macmillan Publishing Company, 1969.

Vin Deloria, *God Is Red: A Native View of Religion*, New York: Putnam Publishing Group, 1973

William Marder, *Indians In The Americas, The Untold Story,* www.thebooktree.com, San Diego, CA, 2005.

Where White Men Fear to Tread: The Autobiography of Russell Means, New York, St. Martin's Press, 1995.

Mary Crow Dog, *Lakota Woman,* New York: Grove Weidenfeld, 1990.

Nora Gallagher & Lisa Meyers, editors. *Tools for Grassroot Activists*, Patagonia, paperback & e-book, 2016.

THE PHILOSOPHY OF THE SEVENTH GENERATION

The Seventh Generation Principle is to think seven generations ahead (about 140 years into the future) and decide whether the decisions made today would benefit the children seven generations into the future.

The first recorded concepts of the Seventh Generation Principle date back to the writing of "The Great Law of Iroquois Confederacy." Although the actual date is undetermined, the range of conjectures place its writing anywhere from 1142 to 1500 AD. The Great Law of Iroquois Confederacy formed the political, ceremonial, and social fabric of the Five Nation Confederacy (later Six). It is also credited as being a contributing influence on the American Constitution, due to Benjamin Franklin's great respect for the Iroquois system of government; which in itself is interesting from the perspective that the United States formed their Constitution, not on the principles of European governments, but rather on that of a people considered
"savages."

The Seventh Generation Principle today is generally referred to in regards to decisions being made about our energy, water, and natural resources; and ensuring that those decisions are sustainable for seven generations in the future. But it can also be applied to relationships. Every decision should result in sustainable relationships seven generations into the future.

NOTES TO THE TEXT

1. William Marder, *Indians In the Americas, The Untold Story,* 2005, The Book Tree, San Diego, CA. Page 1 and note 2 gives a detailed explanation of why the name American Indian is used.

2. J.M. Cooper, *The Northern Algonquin Supreme Being,* Washington D. C., covers primitive religions, No.6, 1933, pp. 3-4, 41,111. Ruth M. Underhill, *Red Man's Religion,* 1971, University Press of Chicago. William Marder, *Indians In the Americas, The Untold Story*, 2005, The Book Tree, "Religion of the Indian," pp. 109-115.

3. M.E. Sharpe, *Shamanism, Soviet Studies of Tradition Religion in Siberia and Central Asia,* Armonk, N.Y., 1990, see also William S. Lyon, *Encyclopedia of Native American Shamanism: Sacred Ceremonies of North America,* Santa Barbara, CA. William S. Lyon, *Encyclopedia of Native American Healing,* W. W. Norton and Company, NY, 1998. Michael J. Winkelman, *Shamans, Priests and Witches: A Cross-Cultural Study of Magic-Religious Practitioners,* Arizona State University Anthropological Research papers, January 1992. *The Sacred Pipe: Black Elk's Account of the Seven Rites of the Oglala Sioux*, Black Elk, Oglala Sioux, with Joseph Epes Brown.

4. *We Have a Religion: The 1920s Pueblo Indian Dance Controversy and American Religious Freedom*, Tisa Wenger, May 1, 2009, University of North Carolina Press. Christopher Vacsey, *Handbook of American Indian Religious Freedom*, New York: Crossroad Press, 1991. 1994 Amendments to the American Indian Religious Freedom Act of 1978. *Bury My Heart at Wounded Knee,* 1970, New York: Holt, Rinehart & Winston. Martin Gitlin, *Wounded Knee Massacre*, 2010, Abc-Clio, incorporated, Timeline of events.

5. Ken Cohen, *Honoring the Medicine: The Essential Guide to Native American Healing*, Ballantine Books; Reprint edition, June 27, 2006. Doug Boyd, *Mad Bear: Spirit, Healing, and the Sacred in the Life of a Native American Medicine Man*, December 1, 1994, Touchstone.

6. https://en.wikipedia.org/wiki/Anishinaabe_clan_system, John Reed Swanton, *The Indian Tribes of North America,* January 1, 1952, Genealogical Publishing.

7. Linda Van Bibber, Manataka American Indian Council, *What Is Your Spirit Name?,* Volume XII, Issue 4, April, 2008.

8. Bobbie Kalman, *Native Homes, Nations of North America*, Crabtree Publishing Company, April 20, 2001.

9. Carolyn Niethammer, *American Indian Food and Lore*, 1974, New York: Simon & Schuster Macmillan Company; Linda Murray Berzok, *Food in American History*, 1st edition, April 30, 2005, Greenwood.

10. Erik H. Erikson, *Childhood and Society*, 1950, New York: Norton. Joseph E. Illick, *Native American Children*; *Encyclopedia of Children; Childhood in History and Society,* 2004. Encyclopedia.com. 6 Mar., 2016, www.encyclopedia.com.

11. Paula Gunn Allen, *Grandmothers of the Light: A Medicine Woman's Sourcebook,* 1991, and *The Sacred Hoop: Recovering the Feminine in American Indian Traditions,* 1986, both from Beacon Press, Boston. Rayna Green, *Women in American Indian Society*, 1992, Chelsea House, New York. Bea Medicine, *The Native American Woman: A Perspective,* 1978, Eric/Cress, Las Cruces, NM. Patrick Deval, *American Indian Women*, 2015, Abbeville Publishing Group.

12. Leonard Crow Dog, Richard Erdoes, *Crow Dog: Four Generations of Sioux Medicine Men,* January 18th 1996, Harper Perennial. Russell Means (Author), Marvin Wolf (Author), *Where White Men Fear to Tread: The Autobiography of Russell Means,* 1995, St. Martin's Griffin.

13. Uta Ranke-Heinemann, "Female Blood: The Ancient Taboo and its Christian Consequences', from *Eunuchs for Heaven*, André Deutsch, London, 1990, pp. 12-17. https://en.wikipedia.org/wiki/Menstrual_taboo (for info on other religions beliefs on menstruation.)

14. Leslie Gourse, *Native American Courtship and Marriage Traditions,* 1999, Hippocrene Books, SC. On love, courtship, marriage and family traditions among several North American tribes, including the Hopi, Navajo, Iroquois, and Oglala Sioux.

15. James M. Volo and Dorothy Denneen, *Family Life in Native America,* 2007, Greenwood Press. *American-Indian Families*, International Encyclopedia of Marriage and Family, 2003, Encyclopedia.com, 7 Mar., 2016. Red Horse, j. g. (1980). *Family Structure and Value Orientation in American Indians,* social casework, October, pp. 462–467.

16. Lester B. Brown, *Two Spirit People: American Indian Lesbian and Gay Men,* Binghamton, N.Y, 1997, Harrington Park Press/Haworth Press; B.J. Gilley, *Becoming Two-Spirit: Gay Identity and Social Acceptance in Indian Country,* 2006, Lincoln, Nebraska: University of Nebraska Press.

17. K. Tsianina Lomawaima, *Away From Home: American Indian Genocide,* November 1, 2000. Just saw the movie *Jimmy's Hall* on Netflex, similar story, took place in Ireland in 1920s; David Wallace Adams, *Education for Extinction: American Indians and the Boarding School Experience, 1875-1928*, Univ. Press of Kansas, October 30, 1995.

18. Peggy V. Beck & Anna L. Walters, *The Sacred: Ways of Knowledge, Sources of Life,* Navajo College Press, 1977. Tom and Mark Bahti, *Southwestern Indian Ceremonials*, 3rd rev. ed., KC Pubs., 1997. William Marder, *Indians In the Americas, The Untold Story,* pp. 133-149, 2005, The Book Tree, San Diego, CA.

19. Ken Cohen, *Honoring the Medicine: The Essential Guide to Native American Healing,* Ballantine Books; reprint edition, June 27, 2006.

20. David F. Aberle, *The Peyote Religion Among the Navaho,* 2nd ed., Univ. of Oklahoma Press, 1991. Suzanne J. Crawford and Dennis F. Kelley, *American Indian Religious Traditions: An Encyclopedia,* June, 2005. Sci Rep. on Cannabis, 2015; 5: 8126, published online, Jan 30, 2015.

21. Denise Linn & Meadow Linn, *Quest: A Guide for Creating Your Own Vision Quest,* Hay House; reprint edition, Aug. 1, 2012. Steven Foster, *Book of Vision Quest,* Touchstone; revised edition, January 20, 1989.

22. Cottie Burland; revised by Marion Wood, 1965, *North American Indian Mythology,* New York, NY, Peter Bedrick Books, 1985. Richard Erdoes, *American Indian Myths and Legends,* January 1, 1984. *The Pantheon Fairy Tale and Folklore Library,* by Pantheon. Suzanne J. Crawford and Dennis F. Kelley, *American Indian Religious Traditions: An Encyclopedia,* June, 2005. Explores the religious practices, movements, institutions, key figures and ceremonial systems indigenous to North America, from the pre-contact era to the present.

23. Warren Jefferson, *Reincarnation Beliefs of North American Indians: Soul Journey, Metamorphosis, and Near Death Experience*, Native Voices, 1st edition, March 25, 2009. Charles Alexander (Ohiyesa) Eastman, *The Soul of the Indian* (Native American), Dover Publications, 1st edition, July 2, 2003.

24. J. T. Garrett, *The Cherokee Herbal: Native Plant Medicine from the Four Directions*, Bear & Company, Feb. 28, 2003. Alma R. Hutchen, *A Handbook of Native American Herbs* (Healing Arts), Shambhala, 1st edition, Nov. 10, 1992. Anthony J. Cichoke, *Secrets of Native American Herbal Remedies* (A Comprehensive Guide to the Native American Tradition of

Using Herbs and the Mind/Body/Spirit Connection for Improving Health and Well-Being), Avery, June 4, 2001.
25. Native American Rights Fund (author), *A Practical Guide to the Indian Child Welfare Act,* paperback, 2007. Laura Santhanam, PBS News Hour, *Suicides,* September 30, 2015.
26. Troy R. Johnson, Joane Nagel and Duane Champagne (editors), *American Indian Activism: Alcatraz to the Longest Walk* , University of Illinois Press, October 1, 1997.
Bruce E. Johansen, *Encyclopedia of the American Indian Movement,* 2013, Greenwood.
27. Johanna Brand, *The Life and Death of Anna Mae Aquash*, Toronto, James Lorimer, 1993, pp. 104-105, July 18, 2011. Eric Konigsberg, "Who Killed Anna Mae?", *The New York Times Magazine*, 25 April, 2014.
28. Declassified FBI/CIA/Justice Dept/White House documents on AIM under the US Freedom of Information Act, Feb. 6, 2003.

INDIANS IN THE AMERICAS
by
Wiliam Marder

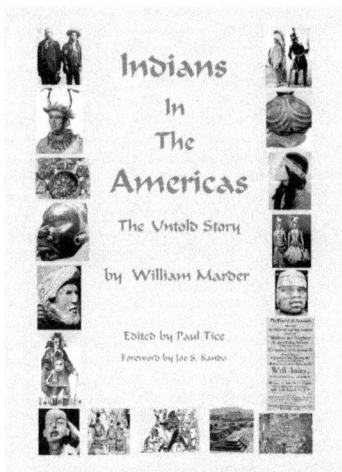

"There have been many books written over the years promising to tell the true story of the Indians in the Americas. Many have been filled with misinformation or derogatory views of the Indian. Finally, here is a book by William Marder that anyone can believe in. It is well researched and tells the true story of Indian accomplishments, challenges and struggles. This book represents years of study and is filled with over 1000 photographs and illustrations. It also contains a complete bibliography with periodicals, along with 780 richly documented, extensive notes to the text to aid the reader in further study."
—Joe S. Sando, Pueblo Indian Author, Educator, and Historian

"The author has spent many years in research and many moons talking with our people. Now he reveals and shares his discoveries with all of us. His words will be an enrichment of educational information for all students reading his book. It will stir your imagination and the historian in all of us. In some cases I found his findings explosive—in revealing facts and stories of yesteryear."
—Patricia Laughing Eyes Holcomb, National President, The White Buffalo Society, Inc.

ISBN 1585091049 • 248 pages • 8.5 x 11 • $24.95
Available from The Book Tree 1-800-700-TREE (8733)
or amazon.com, Barnes&Noble. com or any reputable bookstore

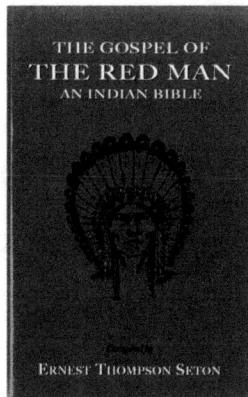

www.ingramcontent.com/pod-product-compliance
Lightning Source LLC
LaVergne TN
LVHW051349080426
835509LV00020BA/3350